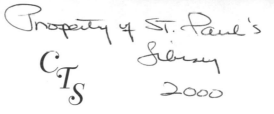

Forthcoming Volumes in the New
Church's Teaching Series

The Anglican Vision
James E. Griffiss

Opening the Bible
Roger Ferlo

Engaging the Word
Michael Johnston

The Practice of Prayer
Margaret Guenther

Living with History
Fredrica Harris Thompsett

Early Christian Traditions
Rebecca Lyman

Opening the Prayer Book
Jeffrey D. Lee

Mysteries of Faith
Mark McIntosh

Christian Social Witness
Harold Lewis

Liturgical Prayer
Louis Weil

Ethics After Easter
Stephen Holmgren

Christian Wholeness
Martin L. Smith, SSJE

Horizons of Mission
Titus L. Presler

Early Christian Traditions

The New
Church's Teaching Series,
Volume 6

Early
Christian
Traditions

Rebecca Lyman

COWLEY PUBLICATIONS
Cambridge · Boston
Massachusetts

The title *The Church's Teaching Series* is used by permission of the Domestic and Foreign Missionary Society. Use of the series title does not constitute the Society s endorsement of the content of the work.

Library of Congress Cataloging-in-Publication Data:
Lyman, Rebecca, 1954–
    Early Christian traditions / Rebecca Lyman.
    p.   cm.   (The new church's teaching series; v. 6)
    Includes bibliographical references.
    ISBN 1-56101-161-4 (alk. paper)
    1. Church history—Primitive and early church, ca. 30–600.
I. Title. II. Series.
BR165.L97   1999   99-22972
270.1—dc21   CIP

    Cynthia Shattuck, editor
    Vicki Black, copyeditor and designer
Cover art is from various sites in Ravenna: Procession of Saints, ca. 560, S. Apollinare Nuovo; Symbolic Throne, 6th c., Baptistery of the Arians; Theodora and her Courtiers, mid 6th c., S. Vitale; St. Lawrence, 5th c., Mausoleum of Galla Placidia; Altar with the Gospel of St. John, 5th c., Baptistery of the Orthodox. Back cover: Angel: Symbol of the Evangelist St. Matthew, late 5th-early 6th c., Archbishop's Palace

This book was printed in Canada on recycled, acid-free paper.

Cowley Publications
28 Temple Place • Boston, Massachusetts 02111
800-225-1534 • www.cowley.org

Table of Contents

The New Church's Teaching Series

A lmost fifty years ago a series for the Episcopal Church called The Church's Teaching was launched with the publication of Robert Dentan's *The Holy Scriptures* in 1949. Again in the 1970s the church commissioned another church's teaching series for the next generation of Anglicans. Originally the series was part of an effort to give the growing postwar churches a sense of Anglican identity: what Anglicans share with the larger Christian community and what makes them distinctive within it. During that seemingly more tranquil era it may have been easier to reach a consensus and to speak authoritatively. Now, at the end of the twentieth century, consensus and authority are more difficult; there is considerably more diversity of belief and practice within the churches today, and more people than ever who have never been introduced to the church at all.

The books in this new teaching series for the Episcopal Church attempt to encourage and respond to the times and to the challenges that will usher out the old century and bring in the new. This new series differs from the previous two in significant ways: it has no official status, claims no special authority,

speaks in a personal voice, and comes not out of com-
mittees but from scholars and pastors meeting and
talking informally together. It assumes a different
readership: adults who are not "cradle Anglicans," but
who come from other religious traditions or from no
tradition at all, and who want to know what
Anglicanism has to offer.

As the series editor I want to thank E. Allen Kelley,
former president of Morehouse Publishing, for initially inviting me to bring together a group of teachers
and pastors who could write with learning and conviction about their faith. I am grateful both to him
and to Morehouse for participating in the early development of the series.

Since those initial conversations there have been
changes in the series itself, but its basic purpose has
remained: to explore the themes of the Christian life
through Holy Scripture, historical and contemporary
theology, worship, spirituality, and social witness. It
is our hope that all readers, Anglicans and otherwise,
will find the books an aid in their continuing growth
into Christ.

James E. Griffiss
Series Editor

Acknowledgments

I want to express my gratitude to James Griffiss for his initial invitation to write this book, and his encouragement throughout. I am also indebted to Cynthia Shattuck and Vicki Black for their patience and editorial skill in the preparation of the manuscript.

The early centuries of the church have always been a rich resource for Christian identity. Anglicans in particular have embraced both the catholic unity of these centuries and their theological creativity. My purpose in this book is to provide only an introduction to the wealth of people, opinions, and places which are the common inheritance of all Christians. The narrative reflects the superb work of my colleagues in the field of late antiquity, but also fifteen years of teaching divinity students at the Church Divinity School of the Pacific in the ecumenical Graduate Theological Union in Berkeley.

As always, Andrew, Kate, and Thomas provided essential distraction and support. This book is dedicated to my parents, the Rev. Howard A. and Janyce V. Lyman, who in their many years of ministry showed that faithful service, spiritual optimism, and critical thinking could be one.

Chapter One

Anglican Identity and Early Christian Traditions

When I was growing up in the Methodist Church, I had never heard of the period of history called "the early church" or "ancient Christianity." I thought between the New Testament and John Wesley was a long period of darkness and decline. When in college I first read about this era in a class on western civilization, I fell in love with its questions, heroism, and passion for God. I delayed my ambitions to study modern theology because I wanted to explore and understand how the religious beliefs of Christianity emerged in these centuries. I am still delayed. Given our own different historical context, what use or authority do these early centuries have? How can we be traditional or radical or anything in between unless we understand how our beliefs and liturgies originated? Becoming a scholar of this period, and then an Anglican, and eventually an ordained priest has been for me an extraordinarily rich way of embracing these historical and theological questions intellectually and spiritually. Understanding our past is essential to dreaming our future.

This book therefore serves as a brief introduction to a foundational era of Christian history. It is offered as an historical appetizer and a theological resource for reflection on our present lives of faith. The first five centuries of Christianity saw its growth from a small group of followers of Rabbi Jesus to a persecuted Hellenistic missionary movement to the imperial church of the Roman Empire. From moving stories of the deaths of young martyrs to violent and intricate arguments over creeds, this time offers a rich and complex heritage for all Christians. It is the age of the "fathers of the church": great orthodox theologians like Augustine of Hippo and Gregory of Nyssa as well as pragmatic and unifying bishops, including Cyprian and Ambrose. It is also a period of great spiritual creativity, from the theology of the Gnostics to the struggles in women's leadership to the profound isolation of the desert monks. Liturgy, orthodoxy, monasticism, and scripture were all "invented" during these centuries. The prayers, hopes, and conclusions of these ancient people are ours whether we know it or not. As modern-day Christians we still speak the language of Roman Africa and Greece, if translated into a different time and place.

Given our diverse religious experiences and institutions, Christians tell this ancient story differently, and find their own thread of ancestors. The Orthodox and Roman Catholic churches see themselves as successors in an unbroken stream of apostolic and spiritual catholicity through the succession of bishops and sacramental life. The Protestant churches may embrace this period selectively—the fervor of its ancient martyrs, its devotion to scripture, its social activism—or ignore it altogether to focus on scripture. In their search for a catholic and reformed church independent of Rome at the Reformation, Anglicans went back not only to scripture, but to these earliest centuries of the church. Here the reformers found a model for liturgy in the language of the people, a learned and pastoral theology, and the shared authority of councils.

Moreover, the present structure of the Anglican Communion, with its independent national churches joined together not by a central authority but by mutual consultation and communion, reflects the unity and diversity of the ancient church. In England, the Americas, Asia, and Africa, we Anglicans sing second-century hymns, recite fourth-century creeds and prayers, and worship according to ancient liturgical forms as part of our contemporary faith. As Christians around the world enter the challenging future of the third millennium, we are returning to the multicultural church of our earliest centuries. In a global communion Christians face persecution, theological pluralism, and divisive questions about authority. Learning from our earlier struggles about unity is an essential part of living through our present questions and conflicts with faithfulness and courage.

ᔐ Tradition and Traditions

Our English word "tradition" comes from the Latin verb *tradere*, which means literally "to hand on."

When we speak of tradition, we mean those things that are passed along from one generation to another as important and essential to our identity. In his first letter to the Corinthians, Paul writes of the gospel itself as a "tradition" that is given to be handed on:

> For I handed on to you as of first importance what I in turn had received: that Christ died for our sins in accordance with the scriptures, and that he was buried, and that he was raised on the third day in accordance with the scriptures. (15:3-4)

The passing on of the testimony about Jesus was the good news. Through the generations, Christians were made by receiving this good news and being united with Christ through baptism. The story of Jesus became their story, expressing the belief in salvation through Jesus that broke the power of sin and bestowed eternal life.

Christians usually distinguish "scripture" from "tradition" in order to emphasize the stronger authority we give to the Bible as the word of God. Yet the Bible itself is the selection of writings chosen and revered by the faithful community. In the second through fourth centuries, oral teaching or "tradition" was a critical test in this process of forming the "rule" or "canon" of scripture. Christians chose their canon from those books of scripture that were in accordance with beliefs and practices, such as baptism and eucharist, received from the apostolic generation. Scripture and tradition are thus deeply intertwined.

At the Reformation *sola scriptura* ("scripture alone") was the rallying cry of those Christians who felt that the word of God should be the only source for doctrine, and the ordering of church life, partly in reaction to the complex theology and papal authority of medieval Christianity. Anglicans affirmed the priority and authority of scripture, but also recognized the continuing role of the community itself as the guardian and interpreter of scripture. They embraced both scripture and tradition: traditions not explicitly sanctioned in scripture could still be maintained. Likewise, for Anglicans today the word of God remains essential, while tradition which embraces the continuity of Christian practice both liturgical and theological is also affirmed.

Just as the Bible is not a single book but a collection of many types of books and testimonies, so tradition is not a single story that we inherit from the past. Just as a family tree is a collection of people who give a particular identity to the present generation, the collection of practices of many Christians over the centuries provide the lineage for Catholics, Orthodox, Protestants, and Anglicans alike. Even when we speak of "apostolic tradition"—the teachings of Jesus that were preached through the earliest missionaries or apostles—we are talking not of a single uniform formula, but of a collection of beliefs and practices. It is a coherent and recognizable collection, but it is not monolithic.

Early Christians used the terms "apostolic" and "catholic" to refer to this core inheritance of the first communities. They defined as authentic and therefore "apostolic" those inherited teachings that could be tested by universal ("catholic") and public testimony. In other words, the true teachings of the apostles were consistent across all the diverse Christian communities. Ancient Christians thus looked to consistency rather than uniformity in order to define saving belief, both orally and in scripture. As we shall see, this early understanding of "catholic" was never intended to exclude varieties of Christian devotion in the apostolic communities of Jerusalem, Antioch, Corinth, Alexandria, or Rome, but rather to guide and ground the existing diversities of practice on a common foundation of apostolic tradition. When we confess a catholic and apostolic faith, we embrace both the historical strength of the core inheritance and the breadth of its rich variations.

Whereas uniformity requires enforcement, consistency demands discernment. Discernment is a more complicated task, requiring that we recognize the fundamental similarities beneath apparent differences. Many of the ancient struggles over theology and authority reflect this difficult institutional and personal process. In the early church consistency was tested in the light of the historical precedents of apostolic tradition and the authority of scripture, but also with an openness to the living faith of the present community. So Irenaeus, a leading second-century theologian, wrote in the midst of bitter division and persecution:

> The preaching of the church is everywhere consistent...and receives testimony from the prophets, the apostles, and all the disciples... which having received from the Church, we preserve. And which always by the Spirit of God. causes the vessel itself containing it also to renew.[1]

To Irenaeus and his contemporaries, tradition was not merely a custom to be preserved, but the living continuity of belief and practice of the people of God.

When Christians fell into theological disputes, which they seemed to do so much of the time in these small early communities, intense reflection on scripture, interpretation, custom, and practice would take place. Often, there was no clear guidance to be found in scripture or tradition, so theologians had to create interpretations based on exegesis and reason. In the later centuries the bishops reluctantly gathered together in councils to reach consensus on controversial topics. Most of the time several councils and the shedding of much theological ink was required to find a compromise acceptable to the bishops, who represented the various local beliefs. It took the bishops over fifty years—from 325 to 381—of sending their opponents into exile and working through theological compromises before they could settle the issues around the Nicene Creed. Our ancient creeds are as much a product of compromise as they are of orthodox definition.

Ancient Christian unity in teaching and in practice, therefore, was a continual process, as the churches faced new challenges from the world around them. Only in the fourth and fifth centuries did the authority of Rome begin to dominate, and then mainly in the western church. The Orthodox continued to see tradition as the common possession of all the ancient churches of Jerusalem, Alexandria, and Antioch, with Constantinople the first among equals. The tribal invasions in the west would eventually erase the ancient African voice of Carthage, leaving Rome as the

the sole apostolic see in the west, to be the key to the conversion of Europe. However, behind the central apostolic authority of Rome lies the rich heritage of the east and of Africa. Christian tradition reflected through the prism of history is not a single white light, but a whole spectrum of colors.

～ Anglican Recovery of the Early Church

This history of a diverse and dynamic catholic Christianity had a profound influence on the emerging structure, beliefs, and practices of Anglicanism at the time of the Reformation. Since King Henry VIII styled himself as a Renaissance prince with an interest in the Greek and Latin classics as well as theology, it is not surprising that the recovery of ancient Christianity through the work of educated men such as Archbishop Thomas Cranmer significantly affected the polity, spirituality, and worship of the English church in the sixteenth century. Like others of their day, these reforming scholars saw the ancient church as an authority to cleanse and correct the contemporary church, as well as to deflect Roman Catholicism's exclusive claims to antiquity and truth.

The "unity in multiplicity" of the ancient church offered an authoritative model for an English church independent of Roman authority. Roman Christianity was essential to apostolic tradition, but it should not overrule scripture or ancient local custom Thus, Article XXXIV of the Anglican Church's Articles of Religion states:

> It is not necessary that Traditions and Ceremonies be in all places one, or utterly like; for at all times they have been divers, and may

be changed according to the diversity of countries, times, and men's manners, so that nothing be ordained against God's Word. (BCP 874)

Based on ancient Christianity, Anglicans believed they
had every right to maintain ecclesiastical, doctrinal,
and liturgical autonomy if they could justify it with
reference to scripture and tradition. Using the linguistic and historical tools of humanistic scholarship,
Anglican apologists studied the early centuries in
order to validate their Reformation principles of theological independence, liturgy in the language of the
people, and common access to scripture. Rome, they
argued, and not the reformers, was the one guilty of
theological innovation.

Obedience to scripture through the lens of learning
and early church tradition became the foundation of
Anglican identity during the Reformation. Anglicans
rejected the notion that tradition by itself should be
the foundation for church practice. Standing against
the Roman Catholic position, John Jewel, a sixteenth-
century apologist for Anglicanism, upheld yet quali-
fied the authority of the ancients:

We despise them not, we read them, we reverence them. Yet, they may not be compared with
the Word of God. We may not build upon them;
we may not make them the foundation and
warrant of our conscience; we may not put our
trust in them.[2]

On the other hand, against Protestant objections that
scripture alone had authority, Jewel's contemporary,
Richard Hooker, defended the use of tradition as pragmatic; in his mind respect for the past was the fruit

prudence and wisdom, not obedience.[3] Thus reforming Anglicans embraced those church practices and
traditions of the early and medieval church that did
not directly contradict scripture, and that made sense
in light of the needs and local traditions of an independent English church.

The early centuries of the church were of critical
importance for Anglican liturgical reform. For
Thomas Cranmer, the ancient church offered better
liturgical models than medieval devotions and practices. Thus, he and the other Anglican reformers
believed the Bible and liturgy should be in the vernac-
ular, and accessible to all the people. Clergy need not
be celibate, and communion should be received often
and in both kinds. At the same time, there was evidence in early Christianity for the three orders of ministry (deacon, priest, bishop) in the practice of
absolution, blessing, and presiding. Ancient
Christianity could therefore provide a liturgical middle
ground between medieval Catholicism and reforming
Protestantism.

Wishing to include a broad spectrum of
Reformation theology in a single prayer book,
Cranmer created devotional language that acknowledged, if not encouraged, more than one interpretation. Thus, the structure of the liturgy and the
concept of common prayer itself acknowledged this
diversity of theologies, yet sought to unify it around
a single gospel core. *The Book of Common Prayer* represented a liturgical compromise for a state church, but
its development was also a profound theological step.
Unity could contain diversity. In the prayer book,
Anglican polity and worship reflected Reformation

beliefs and practices as well as an affirmation of reformed catholicity.

In returning to the writings of the first centuries, Anglicans also drew on the spiritual optimism and incarnational piety of the early church. The sermons and prayers of Bishop Lancelot Andrewes, for example, describe a rich theological vision of grace perfecting a good creation that drew deeply on ancient Christian themes. For him the Church of England began at Jerusalem and continued in unbroken spiritual communion through the centuries to his own day. In the hymns of Charles and John Wesley these Anglican themes of sacramental unity and incarnate presence continue, nourished by ancient Christian authors. For evangelical John Wesley the "primitive" Christians were examples and forebears by their zealous life and spiritual experiences. He was not interested in their doctrinal orthodoxy, but in their hearts. In the hymns of his brother Charles we find the influence of Gregory of Nyssa, a fourth-century theologian who wrote of infinite spiritual growth with God:

> Changed from glory into glory
> till in heaven we take our place,
> Till we cast our crowns before thee
> lost in wonder, love, and praise.[4]

~ Modern Anglican Identity

The spirituality of the ancient church had its most powerful effect on Anglicanism, however, in the Oxford Movement. The leaders of that nineteenth-century revival, Edward Pusey, John Henry Newman, and John Keble, looked to the ancient church for traditions and customs to revitalize the English church. Fearful of the growing secularity of the state, Keble and Pusey looked to the earlier centuries to assert the spiritual independence and ultimate authority of the established church. Their studies and tracts stimulated a renewal of scholarly and popular interest in tradition and spirituality. The religious journey of John Henry Newman is well-known; his studies of the ancient church led him to become a Roman Catholic, feeling that, in spite of its medieval vestiges, it was the nearest living relative of the ancient church. John Keble's book *The Christian Year* made a number of ancient devotional prayers and hymns accessible to a broader public, and at the same time John Mason Neale translated many patristic and medieval hymns that remain as standard texts in our hymnal.

In addition to the late nineteenth-century revival of ancient catholic piety in the Oxford Movement, the embracing of critical historical scholarship also contributed to the foundations of modern Anglicanism. "Liberal Catholicism" was the result of an attempt to balance inherited tradition with contemporary scholarship. The nineteenth-century bishop and scholar Charles Gore declared:

> It is the glory of the Anglican Church that at the Reformation she repudiated neither the ancient structure of catholicism nor the new and freer movement. Upon the ancient structure—the creeds, the canon, the hierarchy, the sacraments—she retained her hold while she opened her arms to the new learning, the new appeal to scripture, the freedom of historical criticism, and the duty of private judgement.[5]

Anchored in the authority of an ancient church that embraced both tradition and scholarship, Anglicans of the nineteenth and twentieth centuries could affirm a broad tradition that avoided fundamentalism and affirmed modern historical criticism of the Bible. The present Anglican diversity of Anglo-Catholics, evangelicals, and liberals reflects this mixed inheritance.

This breadth of vision has been foundational for Anglican leadership in the modern ecumenical movement. The Chicago-Lambeth Quadrilateral of 1888, found in the Historical Documents section of *The Book of Common Prayer*, cites the authority of scripture, the witness of the ancient creeds, the sacraments of baptism and eucharist, and the historic episcopate as the basis for Christian unity (BCP 876 877). Anglicans have offered to other branches of Christianity a vision of communion in faith built up by sacramental living and an ordered ministry—rather than doctrine alone as the basis for unity. This means that Anglicans can enter into fuller unity with Lutherans while at the same time admitting a yearning for reunion with the Church of Rome.

Studies of ancient liturgy also underlay the Liturgical Renewal movement of the twentieth century which sought to restore many of the theological and liturgical understandings of prayer and the sacraments from the early church. *The Book of Common Prayer*, for example, offers a form of the eucharist based on the model of the early church, and includes prayers gathered from the ancient tradition, particularly Eucharistic Prayer D. The Easter Vigil and An Order of Prayer for the Evening are likewise services recovered from the early church tradition that had been long lost to modern Christians. Recent movements for adult catechism and baptism also find inspiration in the liturgies of the fourth century.

Finally, the structure of the Anglican Communion today reflects the local autonomy of the ancient church. The Archbishop of Canterbury has a spiritual primacy as the bishop of the mother church, but has no juridical authority over local churches. When the bishops meet at Lambeth, they discuss issues of mutual concern for the health of the whole church, but the decisions are not binding on the national churches. In ancient Christianity the bishops who signed the creed were expected to enforce it; imperial law could be invoked, but bishops also put spiritual or political pressure on one another for conformity. Yet, as at Lambeth, ancient bishops represented local concerns and were expected by their people to remain faithful to those traditions.

The present conflicts within the global Anglican Communion offer the first, if painful, steps toward recovering a true global catholicity that embraces local diversity as a fruit of the gospel. As in the early church, however, the discernment of our common future will not be easy. Although all churches finally have a voice at the table, we remain divided by culture, economics, and distrust. We are rooted in a common apostolic tradition, yet are torn by conflicting interpretations. In spite of this, the Anglican model of national autonomy in ecclesiastical communion offers at least an opportunity for us to move together as one church into the next century. In this way we offer to other Christians a model of honest debate, faithful discernment, and catholic unity which, ironically, is both deeply ancient and radically new.

∿ Conclusions

At the Reformation Anglican reformers looked back to the early church for a model of catholicity that acknowledged national autonomy. Liturgical and theological efforts to create a middle way between Roman Catholic tradition and Protestant biblicism prompted further reflections on diversity even in common prayer. Liberty from dogmatic authority as well as veneration of the past has therefore been integral to the Anglican use of tradition since that time. From the Reformation to the present day, scripture and tradition have been lived out in dialogue with critical thinking. In our church life, we call our bishops to be guardians, but also prophets. We embrace the authority of tradition, but declare only scripture is necessary for salvation. We call priests to be teachers, but we expect laity to judge for themselves.

What is not Anglican is indifference to or ignorance of the past, or the uncritical acceptance of it. This is not the spirit of Cranmer or Wesley or Keble. Heroic modernists or conservatives do not remain long with us. The strength of Anglicanism continues to be its ability to balance the legacy of Christian traditions both ancient and modern, thus embracing a spirituality of wholeness, incarnation, and sacramental growth into God.

Chapter Two

The World of the Early Church

Romans, Jews, and Christians

The first Christian missionaries entered a world that was intensely interested in religion. However, the rise of Christianity as a new and exclusive faith challenged both Roman traditional belief and expanding political power. Scholars will continue to argue as to how the Jesus movement grew from a Jewish sect into an imperial religion in merely three hundred years. Christians may marvel at this growth, but we also need to understand how the early centuries of Roman persecution and separation from Judaism profoundly shaped our theological and institutional identity. In this chapter we will explore the political and cultural context of the Roman Empire as the matrix for the growth of the Christian movement.

~ The Roman World

The unity of the Roman Empire provided the necessary political stability for the early growth of
Christianity. In 35 B.C.E. Octavian, soon to be Caesar
Augustus, defeated Mark Antony and successfully
established the Roman Empire around the entire rim
of the Mediterranean Sea. This Roman expansion rested on the earlier political unification of Alexander the
Great: three centuries earlier, in 330 B.C.E., he had
established an extensive empire that included and
united the cultures around the Mediterranean from
Greece and Turkey to Israel, Egypt, and Persia. After
Alexander's death, his Greek generals divided his
empire and continued to use Greek power and culture
to rule the conquered areas. This mixture of ancient
local culture and Greek ideals produced what became
known as the Hellenistic age. The Roman dominance
of the Mediterranean world under Caesar Augustus
was therefore only the most recent imperial veneer
over a variety of local cultures in Greece, Carthage,
Egypt, Palestine, and Asia Minor. Possessing distinct
languages and traditions, these localities had been
bound together for centuries through trade, rivalry,
and warfare. Hellenistic Greek, a simplified form of
classical Greek, became the common language in the
eastern end of the empire. This cultural unity made
possible the broad spread of early Christian missionaries as they followed trade routes throughout the
empire.

If the Roman world was knit together by imperial
unity and commerce, it was also sharply divided along
political, cultural, and economic lines. Roman society
was based on a reverence for the past, and resisted

change as disruptive to the ways of the ancestors. Wealth and power were concentrated in the hands of a few: only those at the top of a steep social pyramid could afford the extensive education that gave access to political office. Since wealth was based mainly on land holding rather than trade, fortunes changed hands very slowly. Since some social or economic mobility was available to those in urban areas through education and the military, the cities drew a variety of ambitions and nationalities.

Slavery was an accepted economic fact, but it was not based on race. Highly educated slaves in fact had more power and status through their wealthy households than did poor free people, and they could buy their freedom if they wished. During this time the privilege of Roman citizenship was extended gradually to free males outside Italy; Paul, for example, in Acts 22 surprised his Roman captors by his claim of Roman citizenship, which meant he could expect better treatment. Eventually stresses in the empire would prompt the emperor to extend the rights of Roman citizenship to all free males in the third century. Even so, Roman society remained deeply divided, hierarchical, and status-conscious, with yawning gaps between those who inherited wealth and the working poor. Paul's continued urging in his letters of behalf of equality and unity reflects the deep divisions between rich and poor even when they were part of the same Christian community.

~ *The Gods of Rome*
In antiquity no division existed between political and religious life, and Roman society was sustained by its

traditional piety toward the Greco-Roman gods. The state regulated worship of the gods in order to guarantee their continued protection of the city and state. Individuals or religious movements that challenged these venerable patterns of worship were therefore subject to suspicion and hostility, official persecution, and even death in order to protect the stability of society. Several centuries before, for example, the philosopher Socrates had been executed by the Athenians because of his impiety in introducing new gods. The persecution of the early Christians had a similar cause: it was an attempt by the Romans to abolish a religion that was destructive of traditional beliefs. The political separation of church and state in the United States is in part a response to such persecutions of religious minorities by established state religions throughout western history. After the bitter wars of the Reformation, the legal protection of religious liberty seemed a necessary pillar for any modern state.

Traditional religion was therefore woven throughout everyday life. The great public temples in the center of every city were places where divine intercession was asked to win battles, cement business deals, or ensure a safe journey. At home the intimate household shrines of favorite gods and the custom of pouring out wine as a libation at dinner parties were part of a continuous round of religious acts in Roman daily life. Devout Romans stood to pray with arms outstretched and heads covered, requesting safety, health, protection, or victory. Animal sacrifices were made in order to show devotion to the gods, and the meat sold off for local consumption. Paul's advice to the Corinthian community about not eating meat offered to idols reflects the Christian dilemma about participating in pagan temple activities. Some Christians, including Paul, saw the practice of eating the meat as harmless in and of itself since "no idol in the world really exists" (1 Corinthians 8:4), though he counseled them to "take care that this liberty of yours does not somehow become a stumbling block to the weak" (8:9); others wished to avoid any contact whatsoever with pagan worship.

The vigorous trade and travel of the empire brought a variety of local gods into close contact with each other. For the most part, Roman rulers were tolerant of religions they felt did not threaten their own traditions. Indeed, given the ancient belief in the necessity of divine protection for everyday life, the more gods to be worshiped the better. The gods of other peoples were therefore often welcomed into the Roman pantheon. However, cults that seemed dangerous to the social order had to be regulated, such as the ecstatic mystery cults. The worship of the Greek god Dionysus included festivals of drunkenness, wild dancing, cross-dressing, and general mayhem to represent the underlying chaos and energy of life. Cults devoted to the Egyptian goddess Isis or the Iranian god Mithras grew rapidly in the second century, though their foreignness made them suspect. These cults were not exclusive in belief, but they did require secret initiation and a large fee to join. They remained largely secondary to the everyday observance of traditional religion, but their popularity reflects the cosmopolitan tastes of the expanding empire.

The growing collection of gods with different names but similar powers prompted many to think about the relation of these gods to one another. In the second century many people were "henotheists": they believed one god (such as Isis) ruled the lesser powers beneath her. "Monotheists," on the other hand, believed in the existence of only one god. For henotheists the multiplicity of names reflected many different ways to approach the most powerful god. Thus we have the record of the prayers of Apulieus, a convert to the cult of Isis, as he acknowledged her many names and her supreme power. His initiation and devotion to Isis ensured his utter protection and deliverance from fate and death—something a lesser god could not promise.

Ancient Romans thus lived in a dense spiritual climate of strong powers and divine personalities that could be either placated or offended in the daily round of business and life. The various temples, shrines, and images made access to these gods easy, and encouraged a pragmatic spirituality of petition and intercession. The gods regularly appeared in dreams and visions; they were expected to intervene in daily life. Astrology was important in planning for the future. People wore amulets and regularly made animal sacrifices to ensure divine protection. The countryside and the city were populated with familiar, effective intermediaries, as both educated and uneducated people believed in the spiritual and material efficacy of religion.

∽ *Greek and Roman Philosophy*
Echoing the diversity of religious practice in the international empire, different philosophical schools also offered particular systems by which human beings

could understand the form and function of daily existence. In his satire "Philosophies for Sale," a second-century Greek wit named Lucian captured the competing voices of the Roman intellectual marketplace: dirty Cynics, dreamy Platonists, Aristotelians interested in cash, skeptics interested in nothing. By and large the study of philosophy was a gentleman's pursuit; it was not opposed to traditional religion, but offered a more sophisticated rationale. The diversity of philosophy reflected the cosmopolitan society of Rome as well as an individual desire to understand the meaning of existence.

The dominant philosophical school at this time was a later development of the teachings of Plato: Middle and Neo-Platonism. Reflecting the cultural desire to unify and reconcile opposing viewpoints in the diverse empire, the Middle Platonists created a way of reading Plato that defended the unity of all existence. Life was divided between the perfect, unchanging, transcendent realm above of the divine and rational, and the imperfect, changing material world below of death and the passions. Composed of body and soul, human beings lived on the borderline between the two worlds. They needed to cultivate their mind as a means of communion with the divine as well as to discipline the body and its passions. Platonism therefore expressed the existential tension between the freedom of the mind and the physical constraints of the body. Defining the mind and soul as the superior element, this philosophy sought security and truth in the unchanging spiritual world.

In the third century the Egyptian philosopher Plotinus taught a more extreme version of this philosophy that became the school of Neo-Platonism. Deeply influential on Christian theologians such as Augustine, Plotinus thought that everything originally overflowed from the One, a transcendent first principle. The further a person moved from this first principle, the more life was marked by limitation, chaos, and fragmentation, rather than the infinity, order, and unity of the spiritual realm. Since they believed humans could regain this original spiritual unity by meditation and control of the body, Platonists were deeply religious, and strove by discipline, study, and reflection to gain reunion with the transcendent One through the intellect. Virtue was knowing the good and training the passions to conform to this knowledge, while the body was a lesser good that would eventually be trained by the disciplines of the spiritual life.

These philosophical teachings had a strong effect on the earliest Christian theologians. The Platonic affirmation of divine perfection and beauty was appealing to many theologians, in spite of certain conflicts with Christian tradition and experience. While Christians affirmed the biblical story of all creation brought into being through the will of God, Platonists saw creation as the best possible balance between rationality and chaos. Platonists divinized men of high character and good deeds, but thought the Christian belief in a transcendent God who took on suffering flesh absurd; to them the body and its passions were to be controlled and eliminated, not embraced. For a Platonist, therefore, union with God was ultimately possible, but extremely difficult; for the disciplined few, the mind could be trained for strenuous contemplation of the One. In contrast, for a Christian, union with God by a creature was impossible, yet easy; the gracious incarnation of Christ had transformed and bridged the transcendent gulf. By taking on our flesh, God made salvation accessible to everyone by faith, regardless of knowledge or discipline.

Thus, to Platonists, Christians were uneducated fools, vainly promising the fruits of wisdom and self-discipline to everyone even though these could only be won through hard work and expensive education. As the philosopher Celsus put it:

> The call to membership in the cult of Christ is this: Whoever is a sinner, whoever is unwise, whoever is childish, whoever is a wretch, his is the kingdom of God....I mean, what other cult actually invites robbers to become members!...The Christian god is apparently moved by feelings of pity and compassion for the sort of people that hang about the Christian churches...I doubt very much that any really intelligent man believes these doctrines of Christians, for to believe them would require one to ignore the sort of unintelligent and uneducated people who are persuaded by it.[1]

If Platonism provided a way of understanding the mysterious tension between mind and body, Stoicism focused on problems of self-discipline and nature. Rejecting the Platonist's hierarchy of spirit and matter, Stoic teachers defended the physical unity of all existence. All being was a mixture of spirit and matter, held together by varieties of "tension" or energy. Virtue in some sense was the restoration of harmony between the self and the universe. Roman Stoics such as Seneca and Epictetus thus taught the importance of self-mastery, duty, and submission to providence or fate. The emperor Marcus Aurelius wrote his famous meditations as private reflections on the need for disciplined moral choice, and duty to the common good.

Stoic ethics were deeply influential upon emerging Christian thought because of their defense of providence, subtle reflections on self-discipline, and affirmation of the unity of humanity and divinity. However, because the Stoics emphasized control of the emotions as part of self-mastery and discipline, Christians could sometimes appear as hysterical or obstinate in their joy in suffering and defense of Christ's passion. Yet Christians adopted the Stoic language of discipline, while also stressing human choice and transformation. Thus Origen, a philosophical Christian teacher, borrowed images about cosmic unity to show how Christians would be unified with God:

> The Stoics say that when the element...becomes dominant,...all things change into fire. But we believe that at some time the Logos...will have remodelled every soul to his own perfection, when each simply by the exercise of his freedom will choose what the Logos wills.[2]

For both the sophisticated and the uneducated, therefore, the religious quest revolved around this philosophical tension between soul and body, flesh and spirit. Just as our own language is sprinkled with the language of psychology, so second-century people wondered about fate, contemplation, and free will in the philosophical vocabulary of their day. If the gods are lofty and beyond our knowledge, how do they interact with us as material beings? Where does evil come from? If fate controls all outcomes, are we powerless to change our lives? In response to these questions, both Christians and philosophers defended human freedom and responsibility: the stars do not determine history, for it is open to human struggle. Christians, however, offered the most radical possibility of human transformation for all kinds of people: through baptism anyone could receive new life and spiritual power to live in accordance with divine will through the grace of Jesus. Within this conservative but pluralistic and polytheistic society, Christianity stood in sharp contrast as a new monotheistic religion that was open to anyone.

Over the next several centuries, traditional Roman belief would be challenged not only by new religions like Christianity and the mystery cults, but also by the social and political turmoil of an overextended empire. After the expansion and relative peace of the first two centuries, severe famine, inflation, warfare, and political instability would create both a spiritual and social crisis in the third century. Persecutions of Christians would dramatically increase in order to enforce religious devotion to the traditional Roman gods in an effort to restore political peace. Since Christians rejected traditional polytheistic worship, in Roman eyes they were destructive atheists and were blamed as the cause of division in cities and families and of losses in battle.

The last great persecutor of the Christians in 303 was a shrewd and deeply pious general, Diocletian, who divided the empire in two and pushed through radical economic reforms to stabilize society. Ironically, the equally shrewd and pious general who followed him turned out to be the first Christian emperor, Constantine, who believed Christianity could restore peace and stability to the empire. He did not suppress traditional Roman religion, but gave immense wealth and favor to the Christian churches. In the fourth century, Christianity and Roman religion existed side by side until 392, when the emperor Theodosius declared Christianity to be the sole state religion and closed all pagan temples.

⁓ Transformations in Jewish Identity

The first Christians were, of course, Jews. That is why for many generations after the death of Jesus, Jews and Christians were not entirely separate either in the minds of observers or in their own. The earliest relations between the emerging Christian movement and Jews remain unclear, but well beyond the destruction of the Temple by the Roman emperor Titus in 70 C.E., Jewish Christians would probably have been hard to distinguish from other Jews. As recorded in the book of Acts, the followers of Jesus, led by his brother James, attended the Temple in Jerusalem and kept the dictary laws.

As we may reconstruct from the letters of Paul and the book of Acts, early missionaries went up the coast of Asia Minor from Jerusalem teaching in local Jewish communities. These missionaries passed through the cities and created Christian communities that continued to grow after they left. Different teachers interpreted the gospel differently; we can see this in the conflict between Peter and Paul in Acts 15 over the question of whether Gentile converts to the Jesus movement should be circumcised and required to keep the Jewish dietary laws. In creating a mixed community of Jews and Gentiles, these missionaries raised profound new questions of religious identity and belief. For some, baptism replaced circumcision as the sign of belonging to the community, while for others this link with Judaism was an essential part of the gospel.

At the same time that these early followers of the Jesus movement were spreading the gospel throughout the empire, all Jews were struggling to find their place in Roman society, where they had an acknowledged but not always respected status. The antiquity of the Jews fascinated some Romans and Greeks, but at the same time their separate identity and customs were viewed with disdain. The practice of circumcision, for example, was considered barbaric and antithetical to the Greek reverence for the perfection of the male body. Settlements of Jews lived in the great Hellenistic cities that flourished after Alexander the Great and they adapted to Roman and Greek political domination in varying degrees. However, as recorded in Hellenistic literature such as 4 Maccabees, Jews often fell prey to political or popular violence because they were outsiders to Greek culture.

Theologically, the God portrayed in Hebrew scripture—whether walking in the garden of Eden or destroying the world by flood—could be seen by philosophers as a crude myth. Since Platonists and Stoics affirmed the rational nature of providence, Jewish claims to a personal and mysterious divine will in creation and history were also seen as false and superstitious. The second-century Greek philosopher Galen wrote that the Jews believed in their god's arbitrary power. Such a belief was offensive to Greeks: if God could do anything, the eternal limits of reason were violated and the heart of the cosmos was made unstable. However, other philosophers defended the Jews. Numenius, for example, saw the antiquity of Moses as the source for Plato: "Who is Plato but Moses speaking Greek?" For philosophers like Numenius the account in Genesis was a profound anticipation of the mysteries of creation. In their theology and religious practices, Jews both impressed and puzzled the larger society.

The destruction of the Temple in Jerusalem by the Romans in 70 C.E. was a cataclysmic event for all Jews, including Jewish Christians. As a colony under Roman rule, Jewish dreams for self-determination were severely shaken by the war with the emperor Titus and later crushed by the failed revolt of Bar Kokhba in 130. The leveling of the Temple destroyed the center not only of Jewish worship, but also of their economy, for the Temple had been central to both Jewish employment and religious identity. In the decades after the Roman wars, all Jews struggled to survive as a people and as a worshiping community. At the same time that early Christian teachers and communities were discussing their relationship to Jewish traditions of the law and cult, other Jews began focusing on the local synagogue as the new center of prayer and community to replace the destroyed Temple.

From the varied first-century sects of Sadducees, Pharisees, and Essenes, Jewish religious leadership in the second century came to be centered in the rabbis, the teachers descended from the Pharisees of Jesus' day. As a result of the absence of the Temple and its cult, focus was placed on scripture and the local synagogue as the place of reading, study, and prayer. In an effort to understand, honor, and delight in the scriptures, Jewish teachers relished debate and interpretation, and created the great collections of laws and practices, the *Mishnah* and later the *Talmud.*

The growing tensions between the followers of Jesus and other Jews in the second century are clearly revealed in the writings of the New Testament: Matthew's gospel portrays Jesus as the true teacher of the law in conflict with the Pharisees, while Luke offers an explanation of the mission to the Gentiles in Acts. In the gospel according to John, Jews are portrayed as willfully blind and hostile to Jesus, in part to encourage Christians to leave the synagogues entirely. Using Hebrew scripture as their own, drawing on the vigorous missions of Jews in the first century, and in some cases continuing to keep Jewish law, Christians only gradually pulled away from overt identification with Judaism. Belief in the divinity of Jesus challenged traditional monotheism, and provoked new interpretations of God's covenant with his people. Although they became outnumbered by Gentile Christians in the second century, some followers of the Jesus movement, in spite of growing criticism, continued to keep Jewish customs and practices.

Because of this overlap, Christians in the second century spent much time discussing their relationship to Judaism. Justin, a Christian teacher in Rome, wrote a long dialogue on the prophets and the life of Jesus in which he justified the Christian use of Hebrew scripture by calling the "New" Testament books the best interpretation of the "Old" Testament. Jesus, a persecuted prophet, was the long-awaited Messiah, the Son of God. From this perspective, those Jews who did not accept this interpretation had lost their inheritance as the people of God and had been replaced by the new Christian community. This interpretation was an important strategy: since Christians were the new voice in a society that valued antiquity, they needed to claim the antiquity and identity of Judaism as their own. Other Gentile Christians rejected all ties to Judaism, including the Hebrew Bible.

As time went on, relations between Gentile Christians and Jews ranged from intellectual and exegetical debate to hostile polemics and even physical violence. As the separation between Christians and Jews widened in the second century, the polemics became sharper even as their cultural and scholarly contact continued. As late as the fourth century Christian bishops pleaded with their people not to attend Jewish synagogues or services. Furthermore, as Christian identity itself became more established, traditional Roman tolerance for the Jews lessened and their legal rights were curtailed in the fourth century under the emperor Theodosius. Ambrose, the great bishop of Milan, argued against rebuilding a synagogue that had been destroyed by Christians; to do so would show support for a "false" religion. The common ancestry of Jews and Christians became well-hidden, and the theological foundation of a violent and consistent anti-Semitism was laid by the end of the first five centuries.

～ The First Christian Communities

In contrast to the antiquity of the Jews or the venerable traditions of the Romans and Greeks, Christianity was a new and unknown religion. In Roman sources Christians appear as a distinct and separate group by the end of the first century. Tacitus, for example, speaks of Nero's torture of Christians in order to punish them for the great fire of Rome during his reign. Christians were guilty of "superstition" in the eyes of the Romans: they held absurd and destructive beliefs that were offensive to the traditional gods. While the Jews had enjoyed some toleration from Rome because of their ancient belief in one God and their rejection of images, the Christians had no such standing. They appeared merely obstinate in their refusal to worship traditional Roman gods, as well as foolish in confessing their belief in a leader who was executed as a criminal under Pontius Pilate. Some authors—called collectively "the apologists"—attempted to write reasoned explanations of Christianity in order to gain religious toleration. Justin of Rome, for example, used Platonic philosophy to explain the universal significance of Jesus as the Word who had inspired the philosophers and prophets. He outlined their sacramental practices and claimed that Christians prayed for the well-being of the empire.

Given their obscurity and perceived obstinacy, why did the Christian movement grow? Part of the answer seems to lie in the close-knit religious communities created by the message and faith of the first apostles.

Consisting of small house churches bound together by belief and simple ritual, these groups were nourished and formed by the teaching of a traveling missionary. Their liturgical life was simple, involving a regular common meal and baptism for the initiation of new members. What gave strength to the community was the combination of inclusive membership and exclusive belief. In contrast to the conservative and socially divided society around them, Christian communities incorporated economically and socially diverse people. This inclusiveness was attractive, but not always comfortable. Paul wrote repeatedly about conflict in early communities because of the diversity of people present: old and young, men and women, Greeks, Romans, and Jews, slave and free. Outside the church, they occupied different social strata; within it, the Roman system had been nullified by baptism. So Christians entered a new life of freedom—and confusion. Later on, they would be accused of sexual and political crimes because of their social idealism and the mixing of persons usually divided in Roman society. Even within the communities they would argue as to whether individual social status had been truly or merely symbolically nullified: should a slave marry a freeborn person? Should women be leaders?

In their social diversity these early communities were held together by their exclusive and costly confession of faith. In confessing Jesus as "Lord" or "Christ" ("Anointed One" in Greek), Christians turned away from the traditional religions of the society around them. Conversion exacted a high cost. Committed to monotheism, they would no longer offer sacrifices or prayers to the Roman gods. This refusal isolated them from normal social and economic life, as well as from public worship. Conversions caused divisions in families as Christians gave their primary loyalty to the religious community: archaeological evidence reveals, for example, that Christians were often buried with other Christians rather than with members of their own family. Given the high stakes of conversion, unity of belief within the Christian community and the truth of those beliefs were critical issues. The communities protected themselves by excluding those who did not agree.

ᨒ *Persecutions*

As Christians gained in numbers, the first sporadic persecutions began. In the first two centuries these were purely local, caused by social friction, economics, or personal accusations. Thus a teacher in Rome was turned in by the angry pagan husband of one of his pupils, while Christians were rounded up in Lyons because they were Greek-speaking immigrants and the public games needed victims. In 112 Pliny, the special envoy of the emperor Trajan, recorded his torture of two female deacons simply for having the name of Christian, although he was unsure what crime it represented. As religious outsiders and disbelievers, Christians were convenient scapegoats in any crisis. As Tertullian commented, "If the Tiber reaches the walls, if the Nile does not rise to the fields, if the sky doesn't move or the earth does, if there is famine, if there is plague, the cry is at once: `The Christians to the lion'!"[3]

Martyrdom at the hands of the society around them only confirmed Christian belief in God's protection. "Pagan" became the Christian label for Greco-Roman belief, meaning "rustic" or "civilian," in contrast to the "urban" Christians or the soldiers of Christ. "Demon" is a Christian interpretation of a neutral word, *daimone*, which simply referred to any spiritual power. They saw the pagan gods not as neutral or harmless, but as evil spirits who would teach falsely and do harm. The Christian records of persecution we have contain a blend of actual court transcripts and rich, symbolic stories of a death struggle between Satan and God. The martyrs were celebrated as those who followed Christ in offering the supreme sacrifice of their lives, while their persecutors were pictured as agents of the devil who sought to destroy the church and thwart God's will. Suffering was embraced as essential to the imitation of Christ, while death was the gateway to eternal life. In the account of her martyrdom, for example, the slave Blandina was made the image of Christ himself in the arena at Lyons due to her faith and endurance:

> For in their conflict they beheld with their outward eyes in the form of their sister him who was crucified for them, that he might persuade those who believe in him that all who suffer for the glory of Christ have unbroken fellowship with the living God.[4]

The burial sites of martyrs became holy places witnessing to the power of God, who had helped the weak triumph over the strength of Romans and Satan alike.

~ Conclusions

The first and second centuries saw not only the rise of Christianity, but the transformation of Roman society and the creation of rabbinic Judaism as well. The intertwined threads of all these stories create a rich history and form the background to the creation of the church in the second and third centuries. In attempting to explain Christian life within the Roman Empire, one anonymous Christian wrote:

> For Christians are not distinguished from the rest of humanity by country or by speech or by dress. For they do not dwell in cities of their own or use a different language or practice a peculiar life....Yet, every foreign land is to them a homeland and every homeland a foreign land.[5]

Defined by their belief rather than by their nationality, Christians did not fit the usual social categories of Roman society. They were drawn from every race, class, and nation in the rich cultural mix of the Roman Empire, ordinary citizens of the empire yet distinguished from those around them by their exclusive commitment to Christ. This singularity subjected them to such persecution and scorn that eventually, by the third century, they were vilified as a threat to the empire itself. Yet at the same time they were deeply part of the majority culture. These early Christians were to be in the world, yet not of it.

Chapter Three

Apostolic Christianity

The Gnostic Controversies

In this chapter we will trace the internal growth of Christianity throughout the second century, from the first generation of far-flung missionary groups to a united international body at the beginning of the third century. The events of this century reveal a fascinating and profound debate on the nature of Christianity itself, now two generations removed from its founder. The question became: What is our connection to events that are now a century old? Some Christians argued for charismatic spiritual experiences as proof of their link to Jesus, while others maintained their inheritance by keeping the dietary and liturgical customs of Judaism. The majority of Christians embraced charismatic gifts such as prophecy or healing, but insisted that these gifts be tested against the teachings and practices passed on by those who knew the apostles.

During the second century the controversies concerning authentic leadership, saving theology, and community unity that began to emerge in the first century became more intense and sustained. Out of these debates emerged the defense of the "apostolic tradition" that became the touchstone for all later Christianity. By appealing to the apostles and those taught directly by them as the true standard for authenticity, Christians believed that they possessed the saving practice and belief of Jesus. This tradition was preserved in three ways: first, by establishing an official succession of teachers, defined as the list of bishops in the early communities such as Jerusalem, Antioch, and Rome; second, by defining a body of basic theological teachings as the "rule of faith"; and third, by collecting authentic ancient writings about Jesus, which came to be defined as the "canon" of scripture.

～ Who Should Lead?

We will look first at changes in the structures of leadership and authority as local communities shifted from small charismatic groups assembled and inspired by traveling apostles to larger, settled communities maintained by local bishops, presbyters, and deacons. In the first century the missions of Paul and others established small communities around the urban rim of the Mediterranean in cities such as Rome, Antioch, Corinth, and Athens. During the first century and well into the second, these "house churches" met daily and weekly in private houses for worship and mutual support. Leadership in these groups was usually based on the missionary who founded them, but it was also shared with the owner of the house where the community gathered. Clear evidence of spiritual gifts for preaching, healing, and prophecy, as well as moral character, was required for leaders. We know about these groups largely from letters written between them, giving and seeking advice about questions of teaching, hospitality, persecution, and conflicts within the community.

The main question facing these new communities was how they were to evaluate the truth of new teachings and the authority of new leaders, especially when these gave rise to conflict in the community. Many communities consulted one another by letter. Polycarp, the bishop of Smyrna, for example, wrote to the church at Philippi at their invitation to advise them as to how leaders should behave in the church; he also journeyed to Rome to discuss different customs about Easter in Asia Minor and the west. Clement, a leader in Rome, wrote to the community in Corinth after hearing that a younger faction had thrown out the older leaders. It is from these occasional letters that we must gather our evidence of the church's theology and community life in the second century, for we have very little physical evidence about early Christianity before the third century.

From these sources we can detect some common themes about leadership in the second century. In antiquity the trustworthiness of a teacher was often linked to knowing who that teacher's teachers had been. The letters of Paul tell us that as early as the first century Christians were arguing over the relative merits of various leaders in a community:

Each of you says, "I belong to Paul," or "I belong to Apollos," or "I belong to Cephas," or "I belong to Christ." Has Christ been divided? Was Paul crucified for you? Or were you baptized in the name of Paul? (1 Corinthians 1:12-13)

These arguments over authentic leadership continued throughout the second century, as Christians several generations removed from the original missionaries were faced with a variety of conflicting interpretations of Christian beliefs. As they attempted to answer the question of who should teach, belief in an authentic succession of teachers linked to the apostles emerged as a means of deciding whether a certain teaching was true. Could a teacher be linked to the chain of authoritative teachers, beginning with one of the apostles? Given the diverse group of missionaries who carried the gospel throughout the Roman Empire, this effort to establish apostolic succession was a mixture of the ideal and the historical. Many cities would not have been able to point to a single Christian leader in the first century. Equally important, teachers such as Justin and Clement claimed to be true inheritors of the faith but had no clear link to personal apostolic instruction that would legitimate their own teaching.

Nevertheless, as Christians were increasingly faced with conflicting interpretations of the gospel tradition, they claimed the historical succession of bishops or leaders going back to the apostles for assurance of authentic teaching. Hegesippus, a second-century historian, tried to piece together the names of all the succeeding bishops in Rome. Later, in his history of the church, the bishop of Caesarea, Eusebius, attempted to provide lists of bishops for each major city in order to show an unbroken legacy for each geographical center. Being able to provide a historical link to a known apostle, it was believed, gave legitimacy to the theology of that individual or community.

An early writer on the importance of the leadership of bishops was Ignatius, bishop of Antioch. In 107 he wrote a series of passionate letters to churches in Asia Minor and Rome, composed as he was taken under guard to Rome for execution. In his fear and hope, he embraced a mysticism of suffering, calling himself the "bearer of God." The church alone, Ignatius wrote, is the true body of Christ, united in spirit and blood by the death of Christ, the Incarnate One. He denounced those who denied Jesus had flesh or questioned the authority of the bishop, saying, "Wheresoever the bishop appears, let the people be, even as wheresoever Jesus Christ is, there is the catholic church."[1] His letters are one of our earliest sources for the authority of one bishop in the community, a structure that would become the norm by the end of the second century. For Ignatius a bishop was a charismatic prophet, a teacher who was willing to suffer, and a mediator between the community and the outside world.

Another important early source for our knowledge of leadership in second-century Christianity is the *Didache*, a church manual that includes moral guidelines for Christian life, liturgical rubrics for baptism and eucharist, and instructions for discerning authentic leadership. Written during a transitional time in the small communities, the manual focuses on the problem of wandering prophets; it mentions the local established clergy of bishops and deacons only at the end. False prophets can be identified because they will ask to stay longer than three days, do not work, and ask for money while in a spiritual trance. Once proven as true, however, traveling prophets were given great respect and latitude: they could improvise the eucharistic prayer while presiding for the community, rather than follow the prescribed prayer of the manual, and were regarded as a valuable source of spiritual wisdom. Thus we already see a distinction between those chosen by the community to do ministry within it (bishops or deacons) and those who presented themselves to the community as possessing spiritual gifts of prophecy or teaching. In the early church these qualities were not necessarily exclusive: Ignatius, for example, was a bishop who also had prophetic gifts. Leadership in the *Didache* was not limited to the office of the bishop, but shared with those having charismatic gifts.

Drawing on the tradition of the Jewish council of elders (in Greek they were called "presbyters"), early Christian communities elected one presbyter or a council of presbyters to lead worship and direct community affairs. "Bishop" literally meant "overseer," and the distinctions between bishops and presbyters were not always clear at this point in time. Either title could indicate a variety of tasks both charismatic (healer, prophet, leader of worship) and pragmatic (discipline of community, money manager). Although by the third century the title "priest" also came into use, it was not used in the earlier centuries, perhaps because of its pagan associations.

Some communities developed a twofold ministry shared by bishops and their assistants, called "servers," or "deacons," while other communities had a threefold pattern of one bishop with several presbyters and deacons. Eventually, in the third century, bishops oversaw the administration of a whole city with presbyters presiding at various house churches. Deacons supervised the distribution of money or goods from the bishop's treasury to the poor of the community. These various ministries were eventually formalized as our three orders of ministry, yet they emerged from a variety of offices and tasks shared in the early community by teachers, apostles, and prophets. Particularly striking is the fact that widows seem to be a separate order of ministry at this time. These ascetic women may be distinguished from actual widows who were dependent on the support of the church. Living in private households, they were sexually continent, prayed, studied, and met regularly with the bishop to advise the church.

Because we see the early church in the light of our own later experience of formal orders of ministry, we may not realize how domestic and personal leadership was in these house churches. In these small, face-to-face communities issues of integrity, moral life, and spiritual discernment were easy to identify and monitor. Most of the pastoral letters that bound these churches together urge humility as well as order, openness to the life of the Spirit as well as loyalty to tradition. If bishops and deacons carried out the administrative and liturgical ministry of the community, spiritual gifts of prophecy, teaching, and martyrdom were also honored within the congregation. A tremendous optimism about the power of the Spirit underlay the life of these early communities.

∽ The Invention of Heresy

The bitter theological controversies of the second century help us to see the pressure points within these small communities of Christians. Because belief and membership were deeply intertwined, these doctrinal conflicts were as much about salvation as about authority within the community. We can see this most clearly when we look at Gnosticism, the major defining conflict of the time whose origins are still under intense scholarly debate. Described as "elitist" by its opponents, *gnosis* refers to the secret knowledge that is given to the saved; those who possessed it were saved from the physical world of illusion and change, passion and death. Salvation meant complete liberation from the physical world and restoration to the original pure spirit. Gnosticism saw the world in terms of polar opposites—light and dark, spirit and matter, good and evil. Because they believed God was wholly transcendent, material creation had happened by accident; it was the work of a lower, evil god. Thus, for Gnostic Christians Jesus had little need of a physical nature: he had appeared in the flesh only to rescue souls trapped in the physical world. For other Christians who began to define themselves as "orthodox," Gnosticism's stark contrast between flesh and spirit denied not only the biblical account of creation, which describes all creation as "good," but also the Incarnation.

However, given the common hierarchy of spirit over flesh in antiquity, it was not always easy to separate Christian Gnostic teaching from orthodox Christian interpretation. The language of apostolic writers such as Paul also invoked notions of a higher spiritual world and a spiritual resurrection body. To clarify matters, therefore, Christians invented the distinction between "orthodoxy"—right belief—and "heresy," defined as a wrong or harmful teaching. In contrast to Greco-Roman or Jewish thought, where truth was continually rediscovered and honed through discussion, orthodox Christians proclaimed one ancient, unchanging belief. This was the apostolic teaching that all orthodox communities had inherited and preserved.

Looking at the writings of second-century theologians such as Irenaeus or Tertullian, we see such theological categories were drawn more sharply than the actual life of the community might permit. Orthodox leaders certainly claimed direct succession from the apostles, in contrast to the secret or philosophical teachings of the Gnostics, but some Gnostic teachers claimed this same apostolic authority for themselves. To cloud the issue further, some orthodox teachers, like Clement of Alexandria, offered secret teachings to their more advanced students. The lines of succession for teaching therefore began to be extremely important: Irenaeus could trace his teaching back to Polycarp and from there to John. How teaching was passed on from teacher to pupil as well as the nature of the teaching itself was the guarantee of orthodoxy.

Since the discovery of Gnostic texts at Nag Hammadi in Egypt, popular scholars such as Elaine Pagels, author of *The Gnostic Gospels*, have romanticized Gnostics as courageous free thinkers in comparison to more "dogmatic" Christians, but this draws theological lines too sharply. In the second-century church, definitions of belief and authority emerged very slowly out of the controversies themselves. A century after Irenaeus, Dionysius, the bishop of Alexandria, told a story about a devout layman in his church who discovered twenty years after the fact that he had been baptized as a Gnostic. And Valentinus, a Christian Gnostic teacher, was active in the Christian community at Rome and almost elected bishop.

Although the language of heresy and orthodoxy created in the second century labeled these dissenters as intruders and aliens, in fact the Gnostic controversies were a family quarrel of profound consequence between opposing sectarian groups who knew how to argue and exclude. From creation to incarnation to human motivation, theologians argued passionately as they sought to justify their own authority and establish true Christian doctrine. Today we can appreciate the theological importance of the debates themselves without necessarily accepting their stark contrast of opposing views.

∽ Who is the Creator?

One of the central topics of controversy in this family quarrel was the creation of the physical world. Rooted in the Jewish traditions of Genesis, Christians believed in one God as creator and ruler of the world. This belief in one God not only marked Christians at baptism, but also led them to their deaths when they refused to sacrifice to the gods of the Romans. However, according to the Gnostic Christian text *The Gospel of Truth*, creation by God was an accident by a lower god that trapped human beings in a physical world of change and decay. According to the Gnostic interpretation, salvation would come when the immortal and divine Savior delivered us from this earthly existence, and brought us home to the spiritual world of unchanging perfection:

> Having made punishments and tortures cease...he became a way for those who were lost and knowledge for those who were ignorant, a discovery for those who were searching, and a support for those who were wavering.[2]

Anyone searching to explain evil in the world can understand the Gnostic interpretation of Genesis. If a good and all-powerful God created and controls this world, why is it so violent, uncertain, and dangerous? Roman philosophy assumed a similar tension between a higher, perfect spiritual world and a lower, changing physical world. This tension can be found even within an individual, in the conflict between the cool reason of the soul and the uncontrollable urges of the body. Many people felt utterly trapped by the cruel cycles of fate and nature. The Gnostics attempted to explain such tensions by attributing the creation of the world to a lower, inferior god who was also responsible for the violence depicted in the Hebrew Bible. Above this god was therefore the true, transcendent God who would ensure justice and salvation outside the uncertainties of history. For these Christians, Jesus was the Son of this hidden Father who came to tell us that creation was not our true home, but that we belonged to a higher spiritual realm beyond, unknown to previous religious traditions. For proof they depended on allegory, studying the scriptures for a spiritual message hidden beneath the historical events. By these means believers could decode the cosmic path of true spiritual salvation. Gnostic exegetes were particularly fond of Paul's letters, which spoke of spiritual transformation and renewal: "But we speak of God's wisdom, secret and hidden, which God decreed before the ages for our glory" (1 Corinthians 2:7).

In contrast, orthodox theologians like Irenaeus and Justin argued that Christians must affirm the creation accounts of Genesis. To acknowledge God as sole creator of all existence is to recognize God's absolute power to save us. As outlined in the Old Testament, history and material existence are not errors, but the direct result of God's plan. The existence of evil is the result of the fall of humanity from its original communion with God. According to Irenaeus, evil came about because of the immaturity of Adam and Eve, led astray in Eden by the serpent as if they were children. After the fall, history became the means for their growth into full humanity under the guidance of God. In a beautiful image, Irenaeus explained that creation is always under God's care: like two hands working together, the Son and Spirit act continually to bring humanity back into communion with God. For Irenaeus the radical power of God will be seen in the last judgment, when the entire material earth will be transformed into a place of justice and peace. To question God's power to accomplish his will is to believe ultimately in an inferior deity. Furthermore, the proof of that power can be seen in the endurance of the suffering community of Christians.

The orthodox defense of creation was also a defense of human experience as it is lived daily. There was no secret message, no higher hidden order, no better place. Rather than ascending to a hidden heaven, God worked salvation and love in the midst of the physical and historical. Neither nature nor fate can overcome the saving will of God. Material existence was good; history was the long working out of salvation. Far from being made obsolete by the teachings of Jesus, the Hebrew scriptures were important evidence of God's continual care for the world. Optimistic about the supreme power of God, orthodox Christians proclaimed the eventual transformation of the world through creation, incarnation, and the final judgment and resurrection of all.

◡ Who is Jesus?

Closely linked to the doctrine of creation was their belief as to the incarnation of Jesus. Early Christian devotion was marked both by attachment to Jesus himself and by the variety of images and expressions used to understand and adore him. One of the boundaries drawn most firmly in the second century concerned the interpretation of Jesus' humanity. In the Hellenistic world it was quite natural to suppose that if Jesus were a divine messenger, he had no need to embrace human life in the flesh but could merely *appear* to be human. According to some Gnostic Christians, Jesus' flesh was merely an illusion, a temporary means of appearing to human beings in the physical world in order to preach the message of the Father.

In many ways Gnostics were the first theologians to grapple seriously with the problem of Jesus' humanity, and they offered a variety of solutions.

Since for them the body was not important to creation or salvation, it was perfectly logical to see it as a mere instrument for the revelatory work of Jesus. Material being, they thought, was part of the "fog" of human existence; when spiritual reality broke in like sunshine, the fog of physical reality would be burned away. Some Gnostic texts record the suffering of Christ but interpret it in a distinctive way, seeing his suffering and death as part of a cycle of alienation and return. Salvation in Gnostic Christianity is based on a profound belief in deliverance from the physical world and reunion of the soul with the divine:

> Jesus the Christ enlightened those who were in darkness through oblivion....He showed them a way; and the way is the truth....He was nailed to a tree and he became a fruit of the knowledge of the Father....To those who ate it, it gave cause to become glad in the discovery; he discovered them in himself and they discovered him in themselves.[3]

For orthodox Christians, the rejection of these Gnostic teachings about the humanity of Jesus was deeply rooted in their belief in a good creation. Only the fullness of the humanity of Jesus, the divine Son, could bring about the transforming communion between God and humanity. As Irenaeus argued, "For in what way could we share in the adoption as sons,...unless God's Word, made flesh, had entered into communion with us?"[4] Human flesh was not merely the form needed to appear to our human eyes. Instead, by taking on human flesh God was able both to reveal God's nature and to transfer divine power into human flesh. Christ is therefore the "Second Adam," the one who restored the perfection of human nature by his incarnation and at the same time revealed the mercy and love of the Father. Our legacy from orthodox Christians as they debated the issue of Jesus' humanity with the Gnostic members of their communities is the belief that the story of salvation in history extends from Genesis through Exodus to the incarnation to Easter. The readings of the Easter Vigil and the eucharistic prayers we celebrate each Sunday capture this story of God's continuing care through the biblical narrative from Adam to Jesus to us:

> We give thanks to you, O God, for the goodness and love which you have made known to us in creation; in the calling of Israel to be your people; in your Word spoken through the prophets; and above all in the Word made flesh, Jesus, your Son. (BCP 368)

Equally important in orthodox Christianity was the experience of suffering and persecution shared by the community with Jesus. Does our suffering have any purpose if our teacher did not suffer as well? As Irenaeus pointed out,

> But as our Lord is the only true teacher, he is also the true Son of God, who is good and suffers in patience—the Word of God the Father become the Son of man. He struggled and conquered.[5]

The suffering of the martyrs was an imitation of the suffering of Christ. It was not merely the endurance of meaningless pain, but a victory over the world's hostile powers. The steadfast faith of the persecuted proved that God indeed supported the weak in the face of evil and death. This ancient theology of suffering was rooted in a tremendous optimism: the social and physical order will be transformed through the power of the Spirit. The testing and suffering of Christ as truly incarnate thus became a model and encouragement for persecuted believers:

> So the only begotten Son of God, who was the Word and Wisdom of the Father...emptied himself and...became obedient even to death to teach obedience....He first fulfilled in himself what he wished to be fulfilled by others.[6]

Because of their theological optimism, teachers like Irenaeus also rejected what seems to have been a theology of election held by some Gnostic Christians. Within the stratified society of late antiquity, many people believed that their lives were ruled by fate or astrology. Some Gnostic Christians distinguished between those who had been chosen by God to be saved from the very beginning and those who were not. Paul had already discussed the problems of election in his letter to the Romans:

> For those whom [God] foreknew he also predestined to be conformed to the image of his Son, in order that he might be the firstborn within a large family. And those whom he predestined he also called; and those whom he called he also justified; and those whom he justified he also glorified. (Romans 8:29-30)

Since later Christians, including Augustine of Hippo and John Calvin, also affirmed predestination on the basis of Paul, we can see how these Gnostic exegetes may have arrived at their conclusions. The language of election—God had called them from the beginning—helped them explain why some people were saved and others were not.

Whatever the Gnostics may have taught, orthodox Christians followed the Greek and Roman philosophers in insisting on a doctrine of free will and human moral self-determination. Humans are created free in the image of a free and powerful God; they are not puppets, but are responsible for their choices. Salvation history can therefore only be accomplished through the education and transformation by love of these lost and erring, but essentially free and responsible, humans. Grace and free will work together. Thus the theologian Origen argued that Judas was free to repent and return to God even after his betrayal of Jesus; his deepest sin was in fact despair, not believing in the divine mercy and turning again to God for forgiveness. In contrast to the Gnostic language of election and rest, Irenaeus and Origen urged spiritual effort and growth so that all creation could progress into this union with God through the active grace of Christ. Not only human intellectual or spiritual natures would be healed and transformed through the Incarnation, but physical natures would be transformed as well. According to Irenaeus, "The glory of God is a living human, and the life of the human consists in beholding the vision of God."[7] Humans were created for transforming union with God.

～ Defining Apostolic Teaching

In addition to these questions of leadership and theology, consistency of belief across and within the communities of faith was also a pressing issue for Christians in the second century. To show the breadth and truth of orthodoxy, Irenaeus claimed that apostolic teaching could be discerned throughout the empire. Communities who agreed with one another over basic beliefs and biblical interpretation revealed this common apostolic teaching.

The choice of what could be considered the "true" scriptures was an important part of establishing apostolic tradition. In the second century a wide variety of writings were circulating in the communities for public worship and private devotion. These writings included several gospels, letters addressed to Christian communities as well as individuals, transcripts of martyr trials, homilies, and Christian "novels" such as the *Acts of Paul and Thecla*. At that time "scripture" referred only to the writings of the Hebrew Bible. When Marcion, a controversial teacher in Rome, drew up the first collection of New Testament scriptures, he included only Paul's epistles and a gospel of Luke edited to conform to his theology. Irenaeus argued for the four gospels of Matthew, Mark, Luke, and John, and coined the terms "Old Testament" and "New Testament" to distinguish the two types of scripture. The "canon"—that is, "rule" or "standard"—of scripture attempted to sort out which writings were authentic and to be used in public worship. Only those writings that were consistent with the apostolic preaching should be included in the canon, although other writings that were associated with the names of apostles would be accepted as texts helpful for teaching.

Efforts to establish a canon of scripture proceeded slowly, and during the second century the standard probably applied only to books read in public worship. Theologians such as Origen continued to cite apocryphal works in their writings, and literate Christians undoubtedly continued to read them. The first list of New Testament books corresponding to those in our Bible was not completed until almost two hundred years later by Athanasius of Alexandria in 367. Significantly, he also included a prohibition against reading apocryphal works in private. Throughout Christian history the control of sacred literature and interpretation has been an essential part of theological conflict and authority.

At the same time, a "rule of faith" was also emerging as an outline of apostolic teaching summarizing the main points of Christian belief. The letters of John in the New Testament reveal that in his community unity of belief was considered necessary for sharing hospitality and fellowship:

> Do not receive into the house or welcome anyone who comes to you and does not bring this teaching. (2 John 10)

The earliest statements of faith were simple baptismal confessions in which candidates declared their belief in God as Father, Son and Holy Spirit during a rite of initiation, just as we do in *The Book of Common Prayer* today. The Apostles' Creed, which developed later, was based on the baptismal questions of the third-century Roman church. Summaries of faith are also found in the transcripts of martyrdoms that portrayed Christians confessing belief in one God and refusing to sacrifice to the Roman gods. The rule of faith in the second century was not a creed as such, but rather a short summary of the gospel: God as one and creator, the Father of Jesus Christ; Christ as born of a virgin, who died and was resurrected and who is expected to return; and the Holy Spirit as continually active in the prophets and in the community.

Defining the apostolic tradition was therefore the result of a complex process made up of various tests of authenticity. Correct teaching was the test of leadership, and the teaching itself had to be confirmed by historical practice as well as by scripture. By the same token, scripture itself was tested for its consistency by historical apostolic preaching. In other words, Christians appealed to a web of beliefs based on earlier writings, practices, and traditions, yet they tested each of these in relation to each other. Tertullian, for example, defended the truth of *unwritten* traditions by referring to the traditional practices of baptism and eucharist:

> If for these and other such rules you insist upon having positive injunction in Scripture, you will find none. Tradition will be held out to you as their originator, custom as their strengthener, and faith as their observer.[8]

The truth of Christian teaching and practice could be confirmed not by uniformity, but by whether these teachings and practices were found among diverse Christian communities. Christianity was therefore an open and living tradition, tested and confirmed by history and geography. Irenaeus asserted that the consistency of apostolic teaching could be seen in the rule of faith, the succession of bishops, and the canon of scripture:

> The true *gnosis* [knowledge] is the doctrine of the apostles, and the ancient constitution of the church throughout all the world, and the distinctive character of the body of Christ according to the successions of bishops....And above all, it is the preeminent gift of love which is more precious than knowledge [*gnosis*], more glorious than prophecy, and which excels all other gifts of God.[9]

～ Redefining Leadership

If an essential part of the Gnostic conflict was an argument over the credentials of apostolic leadership, the "Montanist" or New Prophecy controversy continued this debate at a critical time. The conflict forced the church to define clerical and scriptural authority even more sharply. Originating in Asia Minor in the late second century, the "new prophets"—Montanus, Maximilla, and Priscilla—claimed to receive direct ecstatic revelations from God. Both charismatic and rigorous, the movement called the church to a stricter discipline in the face of the approaching end time. Troubled by the laxity and self-importance of the clergy, Tertullian of Carthage became a key member. The New Prophecy movement was not unorthodox in its belief, but challenged the emerging consensus about a fixed canon of scripture by proclaiming new prophecies from the Spirit that demanded greater ethical discipline from Christians. Earlier a defender of apostolic and episcopal succession against Gnostic teachers, Tertullian now exclaimed in frustration, "This is the Church of the Spirit, through a man who has the Spirit; it is not the Church which consists of a number of bishops!"[10]

The rejection of this movement and growing criticism of prophetic gifts in general was a significant turning point. It marks the beginning of the end of eschatological expectation and the high regard for charismatic authority in the church. Visions and healings continued, of course, but they were increasingly on the margins. Prophecy now had to be defined as rational; ecstatic possession was greeted with suspicion, if not condemned outright. Later, the authority and participation of women in the New Prophecy movement was also condemned by the church. In the words of one woman, Maximilla, "I am driven as a wolf from the sheep. I am not a wolf. I am word and spirit and power."[11] The movement itself did not end, although its members were excluded from the church and persisted as an independent Christian movement in Asia Minor until the sixth century.

For the most part, the theological arguments against the Gnostics and New Prophets had to do with the authority of competing teachers, rather than the beliefs of ordinary Christians. Yet these methods for controlling sacred writings and their interpretation gradually had an impact on the church as a whole. The sharp distinctions that second-century theologians made between orthodoxy and heresy began to limit the number and range of interpretations that were permitted, which meant that the clergy inevitably became the sole guardians of tradition, thus weakening the traditional community roles of charismatic prophets and spiritual teachers. Yet the repeated warnings of experts like Irenaeus and Tertullian against the dangers of theological speculation may in fact reveal the liveliness of the laity they wished to persuade. Tertullian's famous comment grew out of his attempt to dissuade ordinary believers from asking too many questions:

> What indeed has Athens to do with Jerusalem? What has the Academy to do with the Church?...We want no curious disputation after possessing Christ Jesus, no inquisition after receiving the gospel! When we believe, we desire no further belief.[12]

Overall, however, the definition of authority that emerged from the second-century controversies provided a theological foundation rather than a closed system. Irenaeus, for example, does not exclude women's leadership or prophecy as part of the apostolic tradition, and he may have defended the Montanist movement in Rome. In his outline of worship and belief called *The Apostolic Tradition*, Hippolytus, a conservative teacher in Rome, sets forth correct formulas for church life yet also mentions the presider at the eucharist as speaking freely at the prayers. For Origen, a gifted teacher in Alexandria, the apostles' teaching was only the beginning of our own spiritual journey into God. Questions have been left deliberately open to draw us along in our own questions of faith. Later generations would codify the traditions further, but in the second century "apostolic" meant a living legacy—an accessible, public gospel drawn from the testimony of the whole church. Its underlying multiplicity of communities and traditions became the essential historical and spiritual foundation of the common life in Christ.

～ Conclusions

"They cannot accomplish a reformation worthy enough for the damage they are doing," commented Irenaeus on the Gnostic controversy.[13] Looking back at this major division over Christian theology, especially in the light of modern scholarship, we can begin to reevaluate both the Gnostic Christians and the orthodox church. Christians inherited the Hellenistic uneasiness about flesh and spirit, both within themselves and in the world around them. With profound insight and skill, the Gnostic exegetes attempted to explain this tension and sense of alienation through a complex cosmology that celebrated salvation through the revelation of Jesus. The Gnostics can therefore be seen as both charismatic teachers and incisive interpreters of scripture, attempting to explain the teachings of Christianity.

However, the rejection of Gnostic interpretations kept orthodox Christian communities in continuity with the historical and moral worlds of Hebrew scripture. The doctrine of "creation from nothing" was in fact one that resulted from Christian arguments with Gnostics; it was also adopted by Jewish rabbis for the interpretation of Genesis. Belief in creation as good ensured an interpretation of incarnation and salvation that included the physical world. This is not to say that Christians escaped the mind-body tensions of the culture they lived in, as we shall see in the chapters below, but rather when challenged by a more spiritual reading, they affirmed the goodness of the material world and the true humanity of Jesus.

While the Gnostics are often portrayed as independent philosophical teachers in conflict with the clergy, I think the evidence suggests that the controversy was in fact a contest between competing teachers with different visions of Christianity. Although Irenaeus and Tertullian defended ordinary believers by dismissing the idea of secret knowledge as necessary for salvation, they also preserved their own authority by warning believers against too much speculation. In contrast, Origen weakened Gnostic elitism by inviting everyone to study the scriptures at their own level, confident the Word would instruct and transform all seekers. In either case, the inclusive sense of Christianity was preserved in the community: all were saved and welcomed into the realm of God through baptism.

However, the sharp weapons of heresy and orthodoxy forged in this era are a mixed legacy to us today. In order to preserve the apostolic tradition, the authors began to overlook the multiplicity and rich variety of our past. In time, the charismatic prophets and women leaders would seem to be aliens, if not heretics, rather than the first teachers of the gospel.

Chapter Four

Christianity and Social Crisis

Persecution, Unity, and Holiness

If competing theologies disrupted Christian unity in the second century, problems of holiness divided the communities of the third. This century in Roman history was an era of crisis, including inflation, famine, and continued war on the northern and eastern borders. For ancient leaders, political instability revealed spiritual disorder, so for the first time the Roman government instituted a series of public religious tests to ensure the piety of the empire. Christians were therefore asked to sacrifice to pagan gods, and if they refused, to face exile, torture, and death. The ferocity of the systematic imperial persecutions called into question the basic identity of the church. Could those who offered such sacrifices be forgiven? Was baptism the ultimate act of Christian rebirth? How could Christians stand united in such an atmosphere of betrayal and controversy?

Fighting for the survival of their congregations, bishops like Cyprian in Africa and Stephen in Rome struggled to define sacramental acts such as baptism and penance in ways that highlighted and strengthened the emerging structures of authority and worship. Cyprian was uncompromising in affirming the church as the ark of salvation: "He who leaves the Church of Christ attains not to Christ's rewards. He is an alien, an outcast, an enemy. He can no longer have God as a Father who has not the Church for a mother."[1]

ᐁ Worship in the Early Church

The communal rituals of shared meals and initiation in the name of Jesus had formed the earliest center of Christian life. The early Christian community in Jerusalem had continued its participation in Jewish worship at the Temple, but also met for prayer and worship in private homes. The structure of the earliest Christian services reflect their origins in the synagogue: readings from scripture, commentary and reflection on the readings, and a public confession of sin. In the original Greek, "liturgy" (*leitourgia*) meant "work" or "service" on behalf of God. In their prayers and rituals Christians celebrated the new joining of heaven and earth in one community through the life and death of Jesus. Ignatius urged in his letter to the Magnesians:

> Have a single service of prayer which everybody attends; one united supplication, one mind, one hope, in love and innocent joyfulness, which is Jesus Christ, than whom nothing is better. All of you together...speed to the one and only Jesus

Christ, who came down from the one and only
Father, is eternally with that One, and to that
One is now returned.[2]

Unity in Jesus was thus the foundation for a diverse
community. Gathered together from various social
classes and nationalities, believers witnessed to this
unity by common gestures, prayers, and beliefs,
including the celebration of the eucharistic meal and
initiation through the waters of baptism.

～ The Eucharist

By the third century the sharing of the eucharistic
meal was the central symbol of community unity. A
second-century prayer, which can be found in the
Episcopal hymnal, evokes their faith in the underlying
gathering and redemption of the church:

As this broken bread was scattered upon the
mountains, but was brought together and made
one, so let your church be gathered together
from the ends of the earth into your kingdom.[3]

In the first century Christians had transformed the
Jewish practice of a common sharing of a meal with
thanksgiving to God into the eucharist, the act of
Christian worship in memory of Jesus. "Eucharist" is
from the common Greek word for "thanksgiving."
The early Jewish meals took place apart from the
Temple when friends gathered at table to remember
the acts of God, to offer prayers, and to bless bread
and wine, the elements of sustaining life. From the
New Testament we learn that a tradition of ritual
meals developed from the last meal of Jesus with the
disciples before the crucifixion, as well as those meals

shared with him during the resurrection appearances. The early community met weekly to break bread in remembrance of Jesus and thus by the repetition of the prayers to share in the new spiritual reality of his resurrection. The meal was called by various names, including the Lord's Supper, the breaking of bread, love feast, memorial, and communion. As the liturgical ritual and its theology grew more complex, by the fourth century theologians would refer to the eucharist most commonly as a mystery, or sacrament *(sacramentum)*. These different names for the eucharist convey both its ordinary sense—people gathering together for a shared meal—and the extraordinary spiritual act of the diverse community gathered as one to share in the death and resurrection of Christ.

Some writings give us a few clues as to what these early eucharists actually looked like. According to an early second-century document, the *Didache*, worship took place within the context of a meal; only the baptized could take part, and if any members were at enmity with one another, they must reconcile beforehand. Prayers for the eucharist were written down, but a presider with spiritual gifts was allowed to extemporize. At about the same time, Ignatius of Antioch insisted that only the bishop or his designated presbyter could preside at the meal and prayers. Obviously, different patterns were practiced in these small house churches. Our fullest early account of the eucharistic liturgy in the early church comes from the writings of Justin, a teacher at Rome. He described for Roman outsiders the presentation of bread and wine mixed with water to a "president," a thanksgiving prayer for creation and redemption with a congregational "Amen," and communion given to all present and taken by deacons to those who were absent.

Almost fifty years later Hippolytus of Rome described in full the words and actions of the deacons and the bishop. Our prayers each Sunday are based on this ancient text, including his opening sentence, "Lift up your hearts." The prayers of Hippolytus are quite familiar to us, as they include the outline of the history of salvation and the repetition of Jesus' words of institution. Theologically, we find rich interpretations of this central ritual that enacted and symbolized the spiritual unity and transformation of the community. For Irenaeus, the reality of the eucharist echoed the truth of God taking flesh to regenerate human nature:

> When the mingled cup and the manufactured bread receive the Word of God, and the Eucharist becomes the body of Christ,...the flesh is nourished from the body and blood of the Lord, and is a member with him.[4]

In artistic representations of these earliest rituals, we can see often not only bread and wine, but fish, which symbolized the miraculous feeding of the five thousand as well as the post-resurrection meal in John 21.

~ Baptism

Probably based on the Jewish practice of baptizing new converts, as well as the account in scripture of John's baptism of Jesus, early Christians also used baptism to bring converts into the eucharistic fellowship. In the book of Acts people were baptized immediately after their acceptance of the gospel message

(2:41). Later on, a period of preparation and instruction seems to have been required, in addition to evidence of commitment and proper conduct on the part of those desiring to join the Christian community. Sometimes lasting up to three years, this period of training was called the "catechumenate," from the Greek word *katecheo* meaning "to teach."

Early descriptions of the rite of baptism reveal a liturgy rich in symbolism. The *Didache* instructs both the candidate and the baptizer to fast for several days before the ritual, and to use cold running water as the first choice for baptismal immersion, but still or warm water if necessary. In longer descriptions found in the later sources of Justin and Hippolytus, a common outline emerges: the candidate stood naked in the water, vowed to reject Satan, confessed faith in the Trinity, and was immersed three times under water. After being clothed again, the candidate was anointed with holy oil and received prayer with the laying on of hands. The triple immersion in the name of the Trinity repeated the commandment of Jesus concerning baptism in Matthew 28:19, but also echoed the confession of faith in the complete action of God as Father in creation, Son as Savior, and Spirit as Comforter. In the early centuries people of all ages were baptized, but as a missionary church the majority of converts were adults making a public confession of faith and being "reborn" into a new religious identity. As the church grew in numbers, infant baptism was increasingly practiced as the community began to include second- and third-generation Christians.

In addition to immersion in water that conveyed new birth and the forgiveness of sins, the rite of baptism included an exorcism and a rejection of the evil powers of this world, and an anointing with oil that bestowed the gift of the Holy Spirit. Since early Christians believed that sinful or demonic spirits still inhabited the souls of the unbaptized, converts needed to be exorcized several times, and before baptism people could neither receive communion nor exchange the kiss of peace within the community. The final anointing and laying on of hands expressed the formal reception of the Spirit. Through the separate actions of the entire ritual, a person was cleansed of old sin and pagan identity, and given a new spiritual identity in Christ through the church. Baptism was therefore a passage of rebirth from the external fallen world into the new and Spirit-filled community. After the ritual cleansing of baptism, a person was considered to have a new and forgiven soul, and to be a full member of the Christian church.

We have only a few physical clues as to where baptisms may have taken place. In 1922 French archaeologists began to excavate a buried Roman city in Syria named Dura Europa. They discovered three religious buildings dating from the third century: a Mithraeum, which is a small room for the worship of the Persian god Mithras, a synagogue, and a Christian church. Reflecting transitions in the growth of the Christian community, the church building was clearly a private home that had been modified for liturgical use, with two rooms combined to create an assembly hall. Another room was a baptistery, with a built-in baptismal font framed by an arch at one end of the room. Above the font were paintings of a child-like Adam and Eve standing hand in hand in front of

Jesus as the Good Shepherd. Here baptism is the place of entry into paradise, where one becomes a new Adam or Eve. On the surrounding walls were painted biblical images, including the miracles of Jesus and the women at the tomb, reflecting the powerful acts of God within the community. The church in Dura Europa is our earliest known building designed both for gathering and for baptism, and decorated to celebrate the spiritual reality of rebirth and healing through Jesus.

～ The Daily Life of Christians

Because baptism bestowed a new identity, the challenge for Christians was how to live a new and separate life in a fallen and sinful world. Together with the instructions for liturgical actions we find moral codes reflecting the actions that Christians should take in imitation of Christ and the Father. Writing in North Africa, Tertullian suggests a specific gesture of remembrance and protection: "At every step and movement, every going in and out, when we put on our clothes and shoes, when we bathe...in all the ordinary actions of daily life, we trace upon the forehead the sign of the cross."[5] Other writings contrast what were called the "two ways" of life and of death. Made up of a collection of biblical texts including the Ten Commandments and the Sermon on the Mount, the *Didache* points to worship and charity as the way of life, avoiding astrology, falsity, argument, and pride. The way of death is one of murder, lust, lies, and economic oppression of the poor and weak. This author, however, is both realistic and charitable in his assessment of human nature: "If you can bear the whole yoke of the Lord, you will be perfect, but if not, do as much as you can."[6] A transformed life was therefore evidence of Christian conviction. Justin describes the courage, high sexual morality, and "philosophical" virtue of even the ordinary, uneducated Christian, while Hippolytus specifies the various professions, such as actor, soothsayer, gladiator, or artist, which must be given up in order to be a Christian. These were professions that brought their members into contact with pagan religious practices, and should not be pursued.

These Christian moral codes promoted strict self-discipline and generous behavior for several reasons. First, charity and self-control embodied the ideals of self-sacrifice and active love found in Jesus and the Father:

> They love all men, and are persecuted by all....They are poor and make many rich....Did God send Jesus on a mission of domination and fear and terror?...He sent him as man to men with the idea of saving, of persuading, not forcing. For force is no part of the nature of God...he sent him in love, not judgement.[7]

Christian behavior therefore reflected and revealed the character of God to society at large. As Justin noted:

> Christ exhorted us to lead all men by patience and gentleness....Many have changed...being overcome either by the constancy which they have witnessed in their neighbor's lives or by the extraordinary forbearance they have observed in their fellow-travellers when defrauded or by their honesty.[8]

Second, the behavior of Christians in imitation of Christ revealed them to the surrounding world as the special people of God. Many of the recommended virtues, such as self-control, honesty, and humility, were not particularly "Christian" in themselves; rather, it was the intensity with which ordinary people practiced them that distinguished the Christian community as a religious sect. The pagan philosopher Galen, for example, dismissed Christian "parables" but admired Christian practices:

> For they include not only men, but also women who refrain from sex...and who in self-discipline and self-control in matters of food and drink, and in their keen pursuit of justice, have attained [a rank]...not inferior to genuine philosophers.[9]

Self-control was one of the most important virtues of the Roman elite and was developed through extensive training and philosophical education. Christians claimed anyone could have it through baptism. In the small communities of converts, the moral life was an important sign of unity, purity, and the coming kingdom of God.

Control of sexual desire was a Christian ideal for both men and women in these communities, but caused the most problem with regard to women. In contrast to the Roman moral code, which required marital faithfulness only for women, Christians insisted on fidelity for both husband and wife. In the light of the approaching end time predicted in the apocalyptic literature, some Christians in the first and second centuries embraced lifelong sexual chastity.

Paul, for example, urged his followers to consider his own ideal of sexual abstinence in 1 Corinthians 7. This ideal did not reflect contempt for the body or for sexuality, as is sometimes thought, but rather a single-minded focus on the spiritual life, which included total control of the physical self. In light of the belief in the incarnation, Christian devotion must involve the offering of both the physical and spiritual self to God. As one of the strongest energies, sexual desire needed to be controlled in the same way a wandering mind was disciplined in prayer or the expression of violent emotions of greed or anger were restricted in daily life.

However, given the traditional importance of the childbearing role in Roman society, for women the religious ideal of sexual chastity was subversive. Chastity challenged the traditional values of marriage, and the independence it created could also threaten social order in a patriarchal society. We see some of these ideals and fears expressed in the *Apocryphal Acts*, ancient Christian novels that featured heroines such as Thecla, who turned from her fiancé, to be converted and who followed Paul as a preacher of the gospel. She was harassed by the authorities not only for her faith, but also for her uncharacteristic independence. Tertullian also noted the domestic strife brought by the conversion of women. Could a pagan husband permit his wife to visit other Christians, going from street to street to other men's houses, especially those of the poor? Could he allow her to be absent all night long at special liturgies or creep into prison to kiss a martyrs' chains or exchange a kiss with the brothers?[10] A third-century oracle recorded, "It is easier to write in water or fly like a bird than recall a wife from Christianity."[11] A substantial proportion of converts seem to have been women. Within the Christian community itself we also find echoes of the conflicts concerning these new roles for women, from the lists of women leaders in Romans 16 to the control of the manner of prophecy in 1 Corinthians 14 to the outright denial of women's leadership in 1 Timothy 2.

Filled with the Holy Spirit through the act of baptism, ordinary men and women therefore aspired to be perfect. Given the high ideals of Christian life and the tensions with the surrounding culture, however, it is not surprising that many members of the community could not consistently maintain these requirements. Within these small and spiritually charged gatherings, the question of sins committed *after* baptism took on deep significance: could one sin after baptism and be forgiven?

In the New Testament writings, one who sinned after baptism was to be excluded from communion for the good of the church. Some rigorists, including groups like the New Prophets, believed that the remission of sin after baptism was impossible, while other Christians encouraged acts of penitence such as fasting, prayer, and acts of charity in order to be cleansed of minor post-baptismal sins. However, even these more optimistic Christians believed that the most serious sins—murder, adultery, idolatry, and apostasy— could not be forgiven by the church. Apostasy was particularly heinous: Christians who offered sacrifice to Roman gods betrayed their sole allegiance to Christ. This was the "unforgivable sin" that placed the sinner outside the bounds of Christian community.

Gradually, a ranking of post-baptismal sins and the means for repentance through fasting, prayer, and public confession grew up in the church. Lesser sins were separated from more serious ones. The confession of sins and readmission after acts of penance were public acts, but in the second and third century the actual practices of penance and restitution varied according to community.

The sustained persecutions of the third century profoundly challenged these ideals of Christian behavior. In the second and third centuries suffering in the name of Christ commanded a prestige that overrode most sacramental or moral codes: the "baptism of blood" blotted out any sin. Equally important, the person suffering torture or eventual death was endowed with a tremendous spiritual authority. Imprisoned Christians, called "confessors," were sought out in prison before their death so that their spiritual power might be used for the forgiveness of the sins of others; confessors who survived continued to have spiritual authority within the community. Hippolytus wrote that confessors need not receive ordination to be presbyters; it was clear they already possessed spiritual charisma.

A moving example of such spiritual power and witness has been preserved in the prison diaries of a young African mother, Perpetua, who was imprisoned in Carthage early in the third century. Unbaptized at the time of her arrest, she kept an account of her inward struggles and imprisonment. She was encouraged by her fellow Christians to pray for visions and to share them with those in prison. Perpetua dreamed of a good shepherd feeding them cheese in a tranquil pasture, and of herself as an athlete defeating the devil. Refusing to listen to her father's pleas and forced to give up her infant son, she grew from fear and loneliness into courage and faith: "Whatever God wants at this tribunal will happen, for remember that our power comes not from ourselves but from God."[12]

For Perpetua her central identity was her Christian faith, and she refused to sacrifice to the Roman gods. Along with another young mother, Felicitas, she was put into the arena to be killed by wild animals and soldiers. Even there she remained an example of courage and faith, telling the others, "Remain strong in your faith and love one another. Do not let our suffering become a stumbling block." To the one who wrote the account of her death, Perpetua's remarkable courage was a testimony to the power of the Spirit. In the complete version of her life, we see her as a confessor who forgave sins, relayed visions to the community, intervened among the clergy for their benefit, and symbolized God's power in moments of fear and death. In Perpetua's life and death we see that for the early church, martyrdom and persecution underscored the reality of spiritual power. These ideals for Christian living, along with increasing social pressure to conform, created the context for the consolidation of structures of leadership in the third century.

∿ Orders of Ministry

Although the second century records a number of different names and titles to designate leaders of the communities, third-century documents reveal a consistent pattern of bishops overseeing presbyters and deacons. Out of the second-century controversies with Gnosticism and Montanism evolved a tighter structure of control, stressing apostolic leadership in historical succession instead of independent teachers or missionaries. Teachers and those with charismatic gifts were still considered important within the communities, but the authority of leadership was increasingly defined by apostolic succession, which meant that it was located in the clergy. The local communities were therefore more structured, perhaps larger, and seemingly able to attract more educated men into leadership positions. As the third century progressed, the intensity of social chaos and persecution increasingly challenged the older structures of charismatic leadership and caused a further consolidation of authority around the bishop.

By the end of the second century, a consistent pattern of the three orders of ministry we know today— bishop, presbyter or priest, and deacon—had emerged. The growth of the communities in the third century brought further clarification of titles and division of tasks, as "lower orders" of ministry also developed, including readers, subdeacons, acolytes, and exorcists. The historian Eusebius tells us, for example, that by the middle of the third century the clergy in Rome numbered one bishop, forty-six presbyters, seven deacons, seven subdeacons, forty-two acolytes, and fifty-two exorcists, readers, and doorkeepers.[13] The subdeacons, acolytes, and doorkeepers performed the tasks done at the common liturgy: lighting candles, serving at the altar, keeping out the unbaptized from communion. The presence of so many exorcists highlights the deep concern for controlling demonic powers in the community. Bishops presided at community liturgies, taught, ordained, and administered the treasury of the community. Deacons were the agents of the bishop in caring for the community, looking after those in need and bringing the eucharist to those absent from the assembly. Presbyters also presided at liturgies and taught.

As the power of bishops, presbyters, and deacons increased, they gradually displaced or absorbed the ministries that earlier had been dispersed throughout the community. Widows, for example, were the first "ascetics," living within a community of prayer and study under vows of sexual continence. Because women in the larger society did not have such freedoms, some Christians were increasingly ambivalent about the role of widows. At the end of the third century, a church order instructed widows to stay home and to refrain from teaching doctrine for fear of embarrassment in front of unbelievers. This document is important evidence that the significant role of women in ministry was increasingly curtailed by the fourth century. In this document "deaconesses" were created as a separate order to minister to women; no woman could see a bishop alone without a deaconess. Earlier, of course, the title "deacon" had been used of both women and men.

We therefore have ambiguous but compelling evidence concerning the leadership of women in the early centuries. As noted above, the leadership of women violated the Roman social codes that regarded women as inferior by nature and confined to the home. However, within the early sectarian household churches, authority and leadership were clearly shared with women. The New Testament provides us with a number of references to women holding roles of leadership and ministry. For example, in the closing of Paul's letter to the Romans he commends a woman called Phoebe as a deacon and patron, and sends greetings to other women missionaries such as Prisca, Mary, Tryphaena and Tryphosa, and Julia; recent biblical translations restore "Junia" as a woman apostle in this chapter (16:7), since older translations used a less common male name, assuming the person in question was male.

In the second century only Tertullian and the pastoral epistles explicitly condemn women's leadership, though some historians have seen women's leadership roles at that time as a feature of "heretical" groups and viewed any evidence of women in leadership in that light; Perpetua is thus sometimes labeled a Montanist. This argument is obviously based on the mistaken assumption that women could not be leaders in the early centuries of orthodox Christianity. On the contrary, both the New Testament and titles from other sources testify otherwise. The high number of women mentioned in martyrdom accounts could indicate that they had an official role within the community. However, the leadership of women became increasingly problematic as the house churches grew larger and more formal. By the third century, authors such as Hippolytus and Origen commonly condemn women in leadership positions.

At the same time that criticism of women's leadership became more consistent, other ministries were also modified in the transition from the second to the third century. The author of the *Didache* instructed the community to honor the bishops and deacons as much as the prophets, but later opposition to the charismatic Montanist movement would throw general suspicion on prophecy itself. In the second century confessors were regarded as persons of spiritual power who could be consulted for absolution; by the middle of the third century Cyprian would declare that the power to forgive sins belonged only to the clergy. Earlier, teachers such as Justin or Clement gave doctrinal instruction to Christians; in the early third century, however, the bishop of Alexandria would criticize a teacher, Origen, for preaching in the assembly as a layman. Two of his fellow bishops defended the practice as traditional, yet eventually Origen was ordained as a presbyter.

Clearly, in the third century Christian communities were becoming more organized and centralized, with the power of the clergy prominent. This consolidation probably reflected the growth of the church as a stable public institution needing to develop an orderly process for establishing the functions and succession of its leaders. The clergy were described by Hippolytus in the early third century as those who received "ordination," that is, the special laying on of hands for a particular ministry. It was a rite performed for bishops, presbyters, and deacons, but not for widows, prophets, or teachers. The clergy thus became the official bearers of apostolic succession, a symbol of internal continuity as well as outward authority.

In assigning the responsibilities and powers of the clergy, Roman assumptions were mixed in with Christian ideals. To the outside society, the role and power of a male bishop would have appeared strange because he associated with a community made up of women, immigrants, and the uneducated: the male elite of late antiquity did not normally mix with such types on an equal basis. However, even many Christians thought that only educated male landowners should be elected to positions of leadership; accordingly, the well-educated Hippolytus patronized his rival Callistus as a social inferior because he was a former slave. However, the proper mixture of charismatic insight and administrative oversight was difficult to find in a leader. As an ascetic, Origen criticized bishops for their love of power and their vanity. Gnostic teachers called the clergy "waterless canals" for their lack of intellectual or spiritual authority, while the clergy in turn called these teachers "contentious philosophers" with no interest in community or spiritual life. The third century was clearly a time of transition for Christian communities, as the changing place of the church within society came up against changing roles of leadership within the church.

～ Cyprian: Bishop in a Time of Transition

To understand how the growth of the community and the intense social pressures of the third century changed the church, we turn to Cyprian, bishop of Carthage. His case provides a good example of the transitions from the small sectarian communities of the second century to the more centralized structures of the third century. Educated and wealthy, Cyprian represented the higher social level of men in Christian leadership positions. Bringing a strong sense of Roman order into the community, he made a clear distinction between the people *(plebs)* and the clergy *(ordo)*. While earlier accounts refer to lay people singing, baptizing, or prophesying in the service, Cyprian never mentions such customs. For him leadership in the church was tightly bound up with the purity and sacrificial nature of the Old Testament priesthood, and the clergy were like the Levites, their role given uniquely to one class of people. The authority of the bishop had to be supreme in order to maintain the unity and purity of the church as the community of those reborn in the Spirit.

Cyprian's focus on order undoubtedly came not only from his background, but also from the events of his episcopacy. A year after Cyprian's election as bishop in 248, his Christian community faced intense persecution. Confronted with internal chaos and war beyond his borders, the emperor Decius issued an edict demanding universal sacrifice to the gods of the empire: each citizen must present a paper certifying that this sacrifice had been performed or be put to death. In the face of such systematized persecution, Cyprian went into hiding, while unprecedented numbers of Christians "lapsed" and offered sacrifice to the Roman gods. Afterward, those who had lapsed tried to find confessors who would grant them absolution for this unforgivable sin, and some confessors who agreed with a more lenient earlier tradition did so. Cyprian was against this practice; the confessors, he wrote, were "glowing in faith and strong in courage, but insufficiently grounded in the reading of the word of the Lord."[14] Not everyone agreed: some presbyters accepted these Christians back into the community and were critical of Cyprian's absence during the persecution. However, as the suffering and fragmented community tried to achieve reconciliation, the situation became extremely unstable.

A council in 251 finally decided that forgiveness and absolution would be granted on their deathbeds to those who had sacrificed. To increase the complexity, other Christians had not actually sacrificed but had purchased certificates claiming they had; the council decided that these Christians were to be allowed to receive communion. With a new persecution on the horizon, Cyprian attempted to reconcile all the lapsed in order to hold the community together. At that point the church in Carthage divided into three factions, with Cyprian representing moderate reconciliation, and the other two factions electing new bishops who were divided between greater strictness or relative laxity.

Throughout this process Cyprian had been in correspondence with the church of Rome. The cities of Carthage and Rome were the great centers of the western church and maintained a cautious alliance, sometimes taking different views on critical issues. The Roman church was split over the same question of the reconciliation of the lapsed. In 254 Cyprian quarreled with Stephen, bishop of Rome, over the best way to receive those from the schismatic groups who wished to return to the church. Stephen accepted the baptism of these Christians as valid and so readmitted them with only the laying on of hands to receive the Spirit within the church. Cyprian, on the other hand, denied the validity of any sacramental act done outside the Christian community: heretical baptism was not valid, and thus he maintained that these Christians must be baptized again within the community. Their disagreement highlighted the fact that there were different traditions of baptism in North Africa and Rome. For Roman Christians baptism included both the water bath and the laying on of hands in equal measure to receive the Holy Spirit, while in Carthage baptism could not be divided into separate acts. Only as a whole could it signify the complete rebirth through the Spirit into the community.

To resolve the doctrinal question, Cyprian called for a council. Stephen was due honor as the successor of Peter, but in Cyprian's eyes he also needed to share his authority with a council of bishops. When Stephen rejected the offer, Cyprian called a North African council to confirm his interpretation of baptism. Bishops from the eastern churches in Egypt and Asia Minor were thus drawn into the dispute, which was eventually moderated by the bishop of Alexandria after both Stephen and Cyprian were martyred in the wave of persecution that engulfed the empire under the emperor Valerian in 258. It was finally decided that "schismatics" could be reconciled with the church through the laying on of hands, but baptism in the name of the Trinity should not be repeated because the church affirmed one baptism for the remission of sins. This decision confirmed the belief that the Spirit was the agent of grace, and that grace was not dependent on the moral purity of the baptizing clergy or the community. This position was followed by the Roman church, but was eventually rejected by the North African church.

Throughout these controversies, Cyprian was guided by his belief in the unity of the whole church as the body of Christ. The bishop was the symbol and source of that unity, as he wrote in *On the Unity of the Church:* "The episcopate is one; it is a whole in which each bishop enjoys full possession. The Church is likewise one, though she be spread abroad."[15] The unity of the church guarded the church's purity, which only then reflected the power of the Spirit. When the purity of the church was violated by sin or division, the Spirit was no longer valid or operative within the community. For Cyprian, unity and purity were inseparably bound together in the body of Christ. Here he was continuing the traditional North African view taught by Tertullian several decades earlier. As we shall see in the final chapter on Augustine of Hippo, this tension between the demand for purity and the need for unity would reappear two centuries later, when the church would again be divided, this time by the Donatist controversy.

～ **Conclusions**

The imperial persecutions of the third century tested both the ideals and the structure of the Christian community. As we learned from the controversy at Carthage, clerical authority was the central tool for protecting unity and judging questions of discipline and doctrine. The earlier varieties of ministries were increasingly replaced and consolidated into the three orders of ministry—bishops, presbyters, and deacons. As church leaders came into conflict with each other over local custom or interpretations of tradition, consultation and compromise through the calling of councils were often the response. In the second century apostasy was an unforgivable sin; in the third, with its intense persecutions, a common system of penance emerged that allowed reconciliation with the Christian community, but maintained the church's unity under the authority of the clergy. A real need for order and unity therefore caused the modification of earlier sectarian ideals of purity and charismatic leadership.

Christian unity was thus often a matter of pragmatism, as communities struggled to affirm the ideal of charity as well as purity. However, it was a pragmatism born of the effects of suffering and a sympathy for the reality of human frailty. While in prison, the martyr Saturus had a vision of arguing clergy; as they sat together and talked, the angels instructed them: "If you have any dissensions among you, forgive one another....Correct your people who flock to you as though returning from the games, fighting about different teams."[16] The ideals of Christian community were realized most deeply in the difficulties of their common life.

Chapter Five

Imperial Christianity

The Desert and the City

I n 303 the reforming Roman emperor Diocletian stood on the balcony of the imperial palace in Nicomedia and watched a Christian church burn, marking the beginning of the last great persecution. Yet only a decade later, after many executions and widespread confiscation of property and books, a new emperor, Constantine, would have a vision of the cross and declare toleration for Christianity. Eventually, he would favor it with vast wealth and legal privileges as his own religion. What happened? This dramatic sea change in imperial policy had profound consequences on the history of the church and indeed all of history.

≈ Crisis in the Roman Empire

When the general Diocletian became emperor in 285, the Roman Empire was beset by a number of internal and external ills: invasions by migrating tribal peoples and rival nations on the northern and eastern borders, severe inflation from the costs of constant war and famine, and political instability as Roman emperors were regularly assassinated by rival factions. These events led many to wonder if the traditional gods were still pleased with Roman society and would continue to look after it. At the time of the great persecution in 303, Christians were numerous in eastern cities like Antioch and Alexandria. They had begun to modify existing buildings for liturgical use and developed a complex leadership structure of bishops, presbyters, and deacons. For that very reason, churches and their leaders were easy to find when Diocletian decided to enforce religious uniformity. The sophistication of this final persecution is notable in that the Romans removed leaders and burned books in an attempt to suppress the organization from the top down. As the intensity of the persecution increased, especially in the eastern part of the empire, a great number of people were enslaved, imprisoned, and finally executed. Thousands were killed in rural Egypt alone.

Eusebius, the church historian who observed and recorded these events, notes that the soldiers became weary from long days of executions. From his perspective God allowed the persecutions as a means of testing the church, which had become lax and complacent. As in Cyprian's North African communities earlier, divisions arose as to whether those who had apostasized by performing the required sacrifice might be allowed back into the community. Two sects sprang up over this issue in North Africa and Egypt in the early fourth century: the Donatists in North Africa and the Meletians in Egypt. These sects observed a strict policy of penance and separation from those who had sacrificed in order to preserve the purity of the church.

This period of intense persecution was the backdrop for the rise of Constantine, the son of a successor to the emperor in the west. First acclaimed by his troops as emperor, he began a long civil war to achieve sole rule in both west and east. On the eve of a critical battle in his drive toward Rome, Constantine reported seeing a vision of the cross in the sky. Accounts conflict as to when and what he saw, but in any case, his new allegiance to Christ confirmed and empowered his push to be emperor as he won the battle over his rival, and finally the office itself in the west. In 313 he issued an edict of toleration with his co-ruler that returned Christian property to Christians and ended the persecution.

～ Christianity as an Imperial Religion

Constantine thereafter continued to support Christianity as he fought to become the emperor of the entire Roman Empire. He granted bishops legal status as magistrates, poured vast sums into church treasuries, and built many large churches. Christians were overjoyed at this showing of favor, believing that God had completed this work of conversion in order to establish Christianity throughout the empire. Our modern interpretations of Constantine's motives are more ambiguous: some scholars believe in his sincere, if gradual, conversion to Christianity, while others see it as a pragmatic use of yet another religion to ensure stability throughout the empire. As earlier emperors had added other religions to the pantheon, so

Constantine added Christianity. As a Roman Christian emperor, Constantine would have seen no conflict between these views. Describing himself as a "brother bishop" and "bishop to those outside the church," he clearly saw his rule over the empire as a divine vocation.

Throughout his life Constantine continued to favor Christianity, eventually granting it his open and sole support, although he did not close down the pagan temples. Moving his capital to the east from Rome, he founded a new city, Constantinople. There he built new churches and eventually outlawed pagan rites within its walls; he planned a mighty tomb with himself listed as the thirteenth "apostle." As had many officials who were afraid of compromising the vows of their baptism in carrying out their official duties— especially ordering executions or killing in battle— Constantine delayed his baptism until his deathbed, putting aside his royal purple for glorious white.

Constantine's patronage of the church in giving vast sums to bishops for buildings and relief of the poor established a basic pattern that was followed by his successors. Religious policies were tied to imperial interests in reform and attempts to bring peace and unity to a suffering empire. To an imperial eye, Christianity seemed like a good tool for social unification, especially if the increasing numbers of converts meant it was in fact the true and triumphant religion.

Continuing divisions among Christians over questions of theology and moral purity within the community, however, hindered this imperial program. Hoping for a means to quiet divided populations and promote divine protection, emperors called and funded theological councils so that bishops from different cities could meet and achieve consensus on thorny doctrinal problems. One observer even complained that the roads were clogged with traveling bishops. Emperors were also given the important role of enforcing the decisions of the councils. Finally, at the end of the fourth century the western general and emperor Theodosius declared orthodox Christianity to be the state religion. In a series of laws he limited the rights of Jews and dissenting Christians, and forbade traditional pagan worship. These laws, together with rising popular violence against paganism, ensured the destruction or conversion to churches of most temples and religious sites. By the end of the century Christianity had been knit into imperial ceremony, civic structures, and Roman identity.

How did Christians react to the fact that their faith had become the Roman imperial religion? Constantine's favor on the heels of intense persecution was viewed by most as a sign of God's favor and deliverance. For the bishop and historian Eusebius, Constantine was the agent of God who established the fulfillment of God's reign on earth just as the kings of Israel had done before him. In general, Christians affirmed the imperial policies when they benefitted by them, and opposed them when they suffered persecution. Thus Athanasius, the bishop of Alexandria and defender of the Nicene council, praised Constantius when he supported Nicene policies and opposed him as demonic when he did not. In North Africa the Donatists continually suffered from imperial policies, and therefore saw state intervention as a continuation of Roman oppression and persecution. For the most part, Christians were happy to embrace the favor of the state as long as they felt their purposes were being served, and they continued to look for occasions to transform the culture around them.

∿ The Ascetic Movement

While emperors attempted to stabilize the empire socially and politically, many devout individuals sought escape from social chaos by fleeing to the desert in order to find a closer union with God. One Egyptian farmer heard in church Jesus' commandment in Matthew's gospel to sell all; accordingly, he sold all that he had, put his dependent sister into a convent, and went deep into the desert to focus on prayer. Through the account of his life written by Athanasius and the collections of his sayings, Antony of Egypt became for later Christians the prototype of the fourth-century spiritual father *(abba)*. Escape to the desert was a traditional Roman way to evade family or taxes or the law, but lay men and women such as Antony embraced this social exile in order to confront demons, pray for others, and draw closer to God through discipline and self-sacrifice. Sought out by other Christians to perform works of healing and intercession, Antony conveyed to them by word and sometimes shocking example the wisdom of strength through humility, and the utter love of God's mercy beyond any pride of discipline:

> A hunter in the desert saw Abba Antony enjoying himself with the brothers, and he was shocked....The old man said to him, "Put an arrow in your bow and shoot it." He did. The old man said, "Shoot another," and he did so.

Then the old man said, "Shoot yet again," and the hunter replied, "If I bend my bow so much I will break it." Then the old man said to him, "It is the same with the work of God. If we stretch our brothers and sisters beyond measure they will soon break. Sometimes it is necessary to come down to meet their needs."[1]

By the end of the fourth century, thousands of people had entered some form of religious life, either in the desert and or in urban households. The word "monastic" is linked to the Greek word *monos*, which means "alone"; monastics chose to leave secular life and live alone or in community. They came from all walks of life: Pachomius ran away from prison, Moses the Ethiopian was once a robber, Macrina refused to marry, Jerome was a former scholar. What drew so many people into a life of single-minded devotion? Some scholars see this movement as a reaction to the lowering of standards in a state church or as an effort to replace the ultimate commitment of martyrdom, which was no longer possible. Others note that ascetic life itself predated the imperial church; the flood into ascetic life echoed the overall growth of the church. The ideal of a life focused on prayer and self-discipline had always been part of the spirituality of the baptized, but monasticism went further in its intense focus on constant prayer, celibacy, and social isolation. As the church became increasingly public as well as intertwined with the political and social structures of the empire, the Christian community included many who were called to radical withdrawal into the silence and solitude of the self.

The word "ascetic" means exercise, and these Christians were spiritual athletes who sought to hone their bodies and souls for union with God. Disciplines of fasting, vigils, and constant prayer were tools to train the body and soul in order to focus wholly on the contemplation of God alone. Yet this strenuous life was not meant to glorify the ascetics themselves, but to reveal and receive the gracious love of God into a heart living without distraction. Qualities of humility, charity, and repentance mattered more than physical endurance. Antony described the path to perfection in this way: "Wherever you go, recollect God in your mind's eye. Whatever you do, do it after the example of Holy Scripture. And wherever you stay, be in no hurry to move."[2]

Early patterns of monastic life in community owe much to Macrina, the elder sister of the famous Cappadocian theologians Basil of Caesarea and Gregory of Nyssa. When her fiancé died, Macrina declared herself to be a "widow" and remained at home with her mother on their estate in Cappadocia in central Turkey. Eventually, she and her mother created a celibate household of prayer that included their servants and grew into a "double monastery" of separate establishments for men and women with regular hours for prayer, study, and work. In his *Life of St. Macrina* her brother Gregory described his sister as both a brilliant philosopher and a teacher of wisdom.

Another important figure in the development of early monasticism was the Egyptian Pachomius. He became a monk after being released from prison, where he had been converted by the loving service of Christians. He founded a community and wrote its rule of life, which stressed that the purpose of monastic practice was to grow in the Christlike qualities of charity, humility, and forgiveness. Such qualities were best achieved not alone, he believed, but by living in community. Obedience to the abbot and to other members of the community was an essential part of the rule, yet much of its discipline was based on encouragement in virtue: "If anyone is weak, they comfort him; or fervent in love to God, they encourage him to fresh earnestness....If they find a monk slothful, they do not scold him, but...visit him more frequently."[3]

Not surprisingly, these monastics, like the early martyrs, were held up as exemplary Christians by the society around them. They were sought after for spiritual direction, served as mediators in social conflicts, and revered for the sheer spectacle of their holy lives. The intensity of their spiritual focus made them free agents as they moved outside the established church and social structures. For those who encountered these monastics, their faces were the face of God; Christ was incarnate in them. The collections of their sayings and acts can sometimes read like Zen sayings, a distilled countercultural wisdom acquired by cultivating the love of God through humility, work, and love. Zealous effort was *not* the way: "Let go of a small part of your righteousness and in a few days you will be at peace."[4] Even if the monks were dedicated to fasting, humility and hospitality must overrule this: "It was said of Abba Poemen that if he was invited to eat against his will, he wept but went, so as not to refuse to obey his brother and cause him pain."[5] These qualities, however, did not negate the focus and independence of a life ultimately directed to Christ alone. Amma Sarah commented, "If I prayed God that all men should approve of my conduct, I should find myself a penitent at the door of each one, but I rather pray that my heart may be pure towards all."[6] Groups of Christians went on pilgrimage not only to see sacred places, but to sit at the feet of these exceptional people.

Ascetical life was a strong lay movement, and so the relation of these independent Christians to the hierarchical church was ambiguous and complex. For the most part they chose to pursue their distinctive lives of prayer outside the normal structures of Christian churches, living alone or in groups and often with no clergy. One monastic saying even warns men to "flee bishops and women." As a sign of both their independence and humility, many male monastics avoided ordination. According to legend, Pachomius hid when Athanasius visited so that he could not be ordained against his will. Bishops who numbered significant groups of monastics in their dioceses, such as Athanasius or Basil, worked hard to incorporate them into normal church life and to persuade them to recognize episcopal authority. A measure of ascetic influence may be seen in the fact that by the end of the fourth century most of the clergy were living similarly ascetic lifestyles as part of their vocation. Asceticism—that is, a life of celibacy, physical abstinence, and disciplined prayer—began by being the vocation of a few, but eventually became the norm of clerical life.

Monasticism slowly became a part of the mainstream of Christian institutional life, but with varying patterns. In Egypt, Turkey, and the eastern end of the Mediterranean, monastic life remained largely unregulated, with simple rules of life. Hermits and holy men lived in seclusion and occasionally intervened in legal and social conflicts as judges, mediators, and advisors to bishops and emperors, revealing the accessible yet unpredictable holiness of God. As ordinary Russian people in Leo Tolstoy's stories are transformed by forest encounters with wild holy men, so in the eastern church solitaries were sought out by pilgrims and those in trouble. Like the confessors in the age of persecution, over time these monastic men and women were seen as windows to the holy. Like the saints and martyrs, they became the subjects of the beloved icons of Eastern Orthodoxy.

In the western empire of Italy and France, on the other hand, monasticism was increasingly regulated by specific rules, and there were fewer independent hermits. The political chaos of the west during the barbarian invasions encouraged solitaries to live in community for protection and stability. With the support of Pope Gregory the Great and the later patronage of Charlemagne, *The Rule of St. Benedict* would become the dominant rule of life for monasteries with its emphasis on the virtues of stability, obedience, and routine. Yet even earlier we may note a preference for ordered holiness rather than disruption in the west. The western church preferred its holy figures safely dead and in one location, rather than hermits who arose spontaneously to confront social ills or the ecclesiastical establishment. Over time the cult of the saints flourished under the protection of the bishops.[7]

⌒ The Cult of the Saints

To reconcile the church of the martyrs with those who had once persecuted Christians and were now seeking baptism could be both difficult and glorious. The expansion of the cult of the martyrs in the fourth century reveals that Christians intended to celebrate their subversive past even in its new imperial context. In ancient cities cemeteries were placed outside city walls so that the dead would be separate from the living and would not pollute ongoing life. Although the Christian practice of reverence for and celebration of their dead was regarded by pagans as both spiritually naive and physically repugnant, they continued to hold regular celebrations at the tombs of the martyrs and even expanded the traditional pagan remembrances of the dead into festivals of resurrection. Here, in the presence of the physical remains of the martyrs, was the window to spiritual power. The churches built on top of the tombs of the martyrs were places of regular worship, healing, and pilgrimage.

In the west these places of pilgrimage increasingly came under episcopal control, thus undermining the power of wealthy individuals to possess and control relics: at the cathedral the bones belonged to all who came for visions or blessings. At the same time, these dear dead now lodged under the bishop's altar justified and supported the imperial bishop seated above. In a moment of crisis, for example, Ambrose had a dream in which long-dead martyrs revealed their burial place to him. With ceremony and care the bones were placed beneath his altar. In the west Christians tended to meet their ancestors through the worship space, liturgy, and calendar of the church, though in both the east and the west divine power continued to be revealed in the human faces and bodies of the martyrs and saints. These "invisible friends" ensured that divine protection was intimately accessible even in times of instability and chaos.

∿ Imperial Spaces of Worship

If the ascetics embodied transformations of the self, the transformation of Roman society was made visible in the extensive church building of the great cities of the empire. A new form of architecture was created to replace the house church: the basilica, or "hall of the king." Its rectangular shape was the common Roman form of public building used for everyday business, including royal audiences and legal hearings. Christians adapted these monumental structures by having one apse—a semicircular end that was approached by a long hall, often flanked by columns, called a nave. The chair, or *cathedra*, of the bishop as teacher and presider was placed in the center of the apse, and the council of presbyters sat in a semicircle behind him. During the eucharist the people stood in the nave and gathered around a simple wooden altar placed in front of the bishop. As the liturgy grew more formal, the altar was moved away from the people further into the apse, creating a sacred space called a sanctuary. Eventually the sanctuary was accessible only to clergy, and the altar was raised and made of stone.

In addition to the basilica itself, other buildings were added to a church complex for specific tasks. Baptisteries were, of course, essential: the church was receiving a steady stream of converts because of its new visibility, social role, and imperial patronage. Usually erected with eight sides and set adjacent to the church, the baptistery itself was a symbol of resurrection and rebirth. After a period of instruction, men and women would strip naked and be immersed in water on Easter Eve. Clothed in white and anointed with oil symbolizing rebirth in Christ, they would then be brought into the basilica to celebrate their first eucharist on Easter.

In many churches the tombs of the martyrs were prominent. Some churches, in fact, were built on the site of a martyr's tomb, which provided a focus for worship and pilgrimage. At these quiet places the power of the martyr's death continued to convey healing, inspiration, and solace. Christians had their own cemeteries, or catacombs, from the third century on, and by the fourth, the popularity of these tombs began to draw public attention away from ancient Roman markets toward the Christian churches. St. Peter's tomb and basilica, for example, and not the ancient Forum, eventually became the religious and civic center of the Christian capital of Rome.

Not surprisingly, changes in the size and shape of Christian worship spaces created new needs for liturgy, vestments, music, and books. As churches began to look more and more like the large public spaces of Rome and clerical hierarchies became more complex, the clergy adapted the clothing of secular court officials to signify their differing liturgical roles and offices. Musical specialists were trained to lead new liturgical chants, while hymnody flourished, since all music at that time was unaccompanied. New sorts of liturgical books appeared to help order and assist the leaders: gospel books, missals, martyrologies. Over time these books began to take on a sacred aspect: only the clergy were allowed to read from them, and the books themselves were kissed and carried in procession. Local synods attempted to standardize and regulate liturgical forms and prayers, moving away from the spontaneity of earlier rites. The liturgies of major centers of Christianity like Rome and Constantinople became the standard for certain regions. Liturgical vessels likewise became more elaborate, made of precious metals and encrusted with jewels. Constantine himself donated seven gold patens to the Church of St. John Lateran in Rome, each weighing thirty pounds. Communion was distributed in both kinds, and the eucharist was celebrated several times a week, rather than only on Sunday. No longer the simple prayers of a private gathering of Christians meeting in a house, liturgy now needed to nourish and inspire large numbers of Christians.

The decorations of the new churches and of Christian artifacts in general reveal the blending of Christian belief and Roman art forms. Rich mosaics, plaster paintings, silver work, and stone carvings preserved traditional natural themes as well as an abundance of biblical scenes rendered in classical styles: Jesus the teacher looks like a philosopher, while the eucharist resembles a rich pastoral banquet. Though similar in style, however, the striking images of Christian power are not quite equivalent to imperial iconography. Christ sits on a throne not as an emperor, but as Zeus, the king of the gods. Equally important, he still sits among his disciples as a teacher; they are not required to stand before him, as the subjects of emperors were. These images show Christian power over the old gods and the old world order, but they also convey the humility and intimacy of the kingdom of God. As before, Jesus continues to be represented in many different devotional forms, displaying all the attributes of the old gods: the supremacy of Zeus, the healing power of Asceplius, the intimacy of Hermes.[8]

We have a telling glimpse into the spiritual practices and worship of this period in the travel diary of a fourth-century pilgrim named Egeria. Large numbers of pilgrims like Egeria traveled to Jerusalem in order to see the actual places of Jesus' life. Writing extensively of her travels in Egypt and Palestine to send back to her religious sisters in Spain, Egeria narrated the wonder of visiting actual biblical sites. Ascending Sinai, she retraced the history and geography of Moses. At each sacred site she and her fellow pilgrims encountered monks who acted as guides, leading them in prayers and reading passages from the Bible. Most importantly, Egeria is our source for the sequence of services celebrated in the fourth century during Holy Week at Jerusalem, a sequence that became the model for Holy Week observances in the middle ages and remains so today.

Whether viewing monks or holy sites, Christian piety of the imperial period was intensely physical. God had acted in human history, so the human senses were seen as aids to develop spiritual understanding. The new magnificent church built over the tomb of Jesus, the steady stream of pilgrims visiting holy sites, the many ascetics in the desert—all testified to the triumph and truth of Christianity. The public liturgies now processing through the city streets and the elaborate martyrs' tombs proclaiming joy and deliverance in the midst of death convinced many that the old gods were indeed now silent.

～ Bishops and Civic Life in the Christian Empire

Like the liturgy, the office of bishop inevitably changed in the fourth century to meet the new challenges of a public church. During the economic and social crisis of the late third century, civic life began to suffer as wealthy men no longer chose to display their wealth in acts of public building and administration, but rather withdrew to the safety and comfort of their country estates. Under these circumstances bishops became even more visible and essential to public life because they were the only prominent leaders who remained in the cities; they emerged as spokesmen for the diverse classes gathered in their diocese. Enjoying the patronage of Constantine and his successors, these bishops controlled vast sums of money to distribute to the poor in times of famine or need; they also held the office of magistrate to decide certain legal cases. Thus, bishops took on the titles and prerogatives of Roman power, and many able men who embarked on secular careers of service ended up achieving the highest offices of Christian administration, including John Chrysostom, Ambrose, and Augustine of Hippo.

A successful example of the responsibilities and life of an imperial bishop may be seen in the career of Ambrose of Milan. Ambrose was a high-ranking government official who was popularly proclaimed bishop of Milan even before he was baptized. Once ordained, Ambrose brought all the skills he learned in government service into the office of bishop, especially in dealing with religious factions in the city and in his relationship with the emperor Theodosius. When Theodosius massacred an entire village that had offended him, it was Ambrose who confronted him and called him to repentance. This event would set a precedent for the independence and spiritual authority of the church over the state in the west. Less admirable was Ambrose's interference in the case of a Jewish synagogue that had been burned by another bishop and his monks. When Theodosius ordered that it be rebuilt, Ambrose argued that a Christian state should not fund the worship of unbelievers.

Ambrose therefore embodied the new episcopal ideals of the fourth century: well-educated, well-born, independent, and deeply ascetic. He not only confronted emperors, but also involved himself with the local people of the city through hearing and resolving legal cases. He wrote devotional hymns for his congregation to sing, some of which are still included in the Episcopal hymnal.[9] His extensive preaching included allegorical exegesis of scripture to reveal its moral and spiritual depth. Embodying the best of Roman virtues and Christian practices, Ambrose was the model Christian leader for men like the young and ambitious Augustine of Hippo, for whom he was a mentor.

Another, more tragic example of the career of a well-born and ascetic bishop may be seen in the life of John Chrysostom. An outstanding orator, John was a famous preacher and extreme ascetic when he was made the bishop of Constantinople. As bishop he preached several times a week to crowds of people with varying degrees of Christian commitment. With eloquence and verve John exhorted his congregation on all aspects of Christian life, from theater attendance to daily obligations of prayer. He urged them to high standards of justice and charity:

> Do not say, "It is impossible for me to care for others." If you are a Christian, it is impossible that it should not be so....Do not insult God. It is easier for the sun not to give heat or light than a Christian not to send forth light.[10]

Unfortunately, both his high standards and his sharp tongue offended clergy and laity alike. At Constantinople he did not fit the expectations of a public official in the imperial capital: he did not entertain lavishly and he criticized the empress for erecting a statue of herself near the church. He also sheltered monks from Alexandria who were in conflict with their bishop, and for this he was deposed by a council orchestrated by a rival bishop, Theophilus of Alexandria. John died in exile.

These stories reveal the basic outlines of imperial episcopal life: a prominent civic role, much public preaching enhanced by classical rhetorical ability, negotiation with all levels of society from crowds to emperors, and the defense of Christian orthodoxy. The practice of asceticism was essential in setting the bishop apart from other public officials. As representatives of the church, bishops offered a new vision of social solidarity based on sacramental unity: no longer divided by class or nation, Christian Romans were all part of the body of Christ. The poor were now visible to the elite as brothers and sisters in Christ.[11] As seen in the career of John Chrysostom, however, the social and spiritual responsibilities of episcopacy were complex and difficult to maintain. Neither asceticism nor social class could necessarily save a bishop from political turmoil or ecclesiastical rivalry.

∿ Conclusions

The sea change of Roman imperial religious policy in the fourth century created new challenges and opportunities for a church that had emerged from the margins. With this change in status, Christians brought both their weaknesses and their strengths into their new prominent social role. The fierce theological debates that had always divided and defined Christian communities were now public quarrels. With the vast flood of imperial wealth into the church, diocesan privileges and civic politics exacerbated theological conflicts as did monastic loyalties and parties. Christians therefore carried their own factional disputes into the already divided cities of the eastern empire. Yet the Christian understanding of a single body of Christ made up of people from all walks of life also transformed hierarchical Roman culture. Well-born men and women put aside much privilege and power to adopt a simple life, while lower-class women and men vaulted into social prominence as teachers of wisdom in the ascetic movement. To be an effective Christian leader in the fourth century meant learning not only from Cicero, but also from the illiterate desert Christians.

Yet the question remains, what was converted in the fourth century—Rome or Christianity? Many Christians have celebrated this providential transformation of Rome by the conversion of Constantine; it created a new civilization of classical Christianity. Others have argued that the original purity of the gospel was compromised by state support of the church as the church began to share and uphold the values of the dominant society. Some secular critics have held that Christianity itself was harmful; it suppressed traditional Greco-Roman ideals of political dialogue and destroyed the beautiful temples of traditional religion. Anglicans have characteristically occupied a variety of positions along this spectrum. For some, such as John Wesley, the earlier the period of history, the purer its tradition. For others, imperial Christianity was a synthesis of the classical inheritance and the gospel through the brilliant theology of Augustine and the Cappadocian theologians Basil and Gregory. Whatever our own perspective on these events, the fourth century was a crucible of social and religious change for Romans and Christians alike, setting lasting patterns of law, religion, and culture in western civilization.

Chapter Six

Who is Jesus?

Early Images of Christ

No one hears language in a vacuum: each of us receives the Word of God in a particular cultural context. In other words, our theology reflects the biases and filters of our own time and place. As we look at the first theologies of Jesus in this chapter, we will see how ancient images from Platonism and Judaism shaped early reflections on Jesus' life and resurrection. Likewise, when we look back through the centuries of Christian art, we find many different images of Jesus—the philosopher, the monk, the suffering man, the athlete, the liberator. These images may present strange faces to us today, but they reflect the deepest yearnings of their time. Christians in every generation struggle to express their faith through their interpretation of scripture and the values of their own society and experience. In our present age of scientific inquiry, for example, a group of scholars called the Jesus Seminar uses historical critical methods to get at the "real" Jesus, whom they believe has been obscured by dogma. In antiquity, on the other hand, theologians sought the broadest, most transcendent categories to express for the community the "real" meaning of Jesus' life and work. To describe Jesus in philosophical language was to show his ultimate authority and reality.

In the first centuries the Christian belief that Jesus was God posed a problem for Jewish monotheism: how could one confess two gods and remain faithful to the Old Testament? Jewish Christians had inherited the long tradition of belief in the one God who had created heaven and earth and established an exclusive covenant with the people of Israel. Their religious history included a long battle against the temptation to worship other gods. What could be the relation of the historical man Jesus to the transcendent Holy One of Jewish belief? For converts to Christianity from the Roman world, there was an equally serious problem. According to the traditions of Platonism and Stoicism, by definition God is beyond suffering and change. If Jesus was the transcendent cause of existence, the Word of God, how could he could suffer and die upon a cross? As early Christians struggled to express their faith in Jesus the divine savior, they did so within the images of their culture, both Jewish and Hellenistic. In this chapter we will look at the varied ways in which early Christians translated their experience of Jesus and redemption into the common languages of their time.

～ New Testament Images of God
The resurrection of Jesus galvanized his despairing community into a missionary movement of new

hope. The same disciples who had feared that Jesus' crucifixion signaled the end of his mission now preached Jesus as the risen Lord. To these first believers, Jesus' resurrection ushered in the reign of God. As the first missionaries moved beyond Jerusalem, teaching and baptizing in the name of Jesus, they shared a belief in the universal significance of salvation for Jews and Gentiles: "There is no distinction," Paul argued in his letter to the Romans, "since all have sinned and fall short of the glory of God....Or is God the God of Jews only?" (3:22-23, 29). For Christians, the life, death, and resurrection of Jesus became the new lens for understanding biblical monotheism and God's activity in the world. Seeing Jesus as God's decisive revelation eventually led early Christians to teach a new belief in God as Trinity: Father, Son, and Holy Spirit.

Scripture was, of course, the primary source for early theological reflection on the life, work, and identity of Jesus. For early Christians "scripture" was the Hebrew scriptures, or what we now call the Old Testament. These writings offered many images through which to understand the relationship of the risen Christ to the one God of Jewish belief. The holiness of a single God had been fiercely protected by the Jews and was their defining belief in a polytheistic world. The first commandment given to Moses was a call to exclusive worship of God the creator, and the rejection of all other loyalties as idolatry. This God could be revealed through intermediaries or messengers such as angels, but God alone was divine and all-powerful by nature. In Proverbs one aspect of God's activity was personified in the person of Wisdom, who dwells with wise people and reveals God's law:

> The LORD created me at the beginning of his work, the first of his acts of long ago....Then I was beside him, like a master worker....Happy is the one who listens to me,...for whoever finds me finds life and obtains favor from the LORD. (Proverbs 8:22, 30, 34-35)

As the hope for a Messiah grew over time, it took the form of a savior whose appearance would signal the beginning of the rule of God on earth. By acknowledging Jesus as "Christ"—the Greek word for "Anointed One" or "Messiah"—the early community affirmed that Jesus was the one sent by God to accomplish this salvific work: "In Christ God was reconciling the world to himself" (2 Corinthians 5:19). Originally, the titles "Son of God" and "Son of Man" referred to this messianic role, signaling that the age of the new creation was at hand.

The belief that Jesus was sent from God was interpreted in multiple ways in the Christian community, and these interpretations are preserved in the collection of writings we call the New Testament. The four canonical gospels preserve four early perspectives on Jesus' life and work: the apocalyptic wonder-worker in Mark, the long-awaited Messiah in Matthew, the light to the Gentiles in Luke, and the teacher of wisdom in John. In some of the letters of Paul we can discern early hymns of praise to Jesus, speaking of him in cosmic terms echoing the descriptions of Wisdom: "He is the image of the invisible God, the firstborn of all creation; for in him all things in heaven and on earth were created" (Colossians 1:15-16). Thus Christians began to speak of the saving actions of Jesus as having a universal effect, outside of time or the exclusive covenant history of Judaism. No longer merely a historical, if inspired, prophet or teacher, Jesus was increasingly identified with the Wisdom of God, the agent of creation and revelation. This cosmic universalism was also reflected in the unifying action of baptism: "There is no longer Jew or Greek, there is no longer slave or free, there is no longer male and female; for all of you are one in Christ Jesus" (Galatians 3:28).

The descriptions of Jesus' divinity were always connected to remembrances of his earthly life. His divine significance was therefore read through the lens of his historical life, as seen in another hymn of the early church: "Though he was in the form of God, [he] did not regard equality with God as something to be exploited, but emptied himself, taking the form of a slave, being born in human likeness" (Philippians 2:6-7). The taking on of flesh in the Incarnation echoed the humility of Jesus' self-offering on the cross. Thus the prologue of the gospel of John charts the progress of the pre-existent Word from the creation of the universe to the one who lived among us: "The Word became flesh and lived among us, and we have seen his glory, the glory as of a father's only Son, full of grace and truth" (John 1:14).

The experience of the resurrection prompted early Christians to look back at the life and death of Jesus as signifying more than just another human life: the teachings, radical self-offering on the cross, and res- urrection appearances conveyed the beginning of a new reality, the presence of God dwelling in human history and transforming human nature. While some Christians continued to speak of Jesus as a "prophet" or "teacher" used by God for a special purpose, Jesus was increasingly seen as God incarnate: God had somehow taken flesh and blood in the human life of Jesus. In late antiquity it was not uncommon to speak of gods taking on human form temporarily; nor was it unusual for great and wise men to be called "sons of god." However, Christians used this common language for an uncommon event: the presence of God himself in a suffering human being whose death and resurrection became the decisive and universal event for the salvation of all. This reversal of normal expectations about how God might come as savior was described by Paul:

> For Jews demand signs and Greeks desire wisdom, but we proclaim Christ crucified, a stumbling block to Jews and foolishness to Gentiles....God chose what is foolish in the world to shame the wise; God chose what is weak in the world to shame the strong....He is the source of your life in Christ Jesus, who became for us wisdom from God, and righteousness and sanctification and redemption. (1 Corinthians 1:22-23, 27, 30)

Affirming this decisive and unique role of Jesus raised a number of questions about his relation to the one God. Like other early followers of Jesus, Paul continued to confess his monotheism: "For us there is one God, the Father, from whom are all things and for whom we exist, and one Lord, Jesus Christ" (1

Corinthians 8:6). At the same time, calling Jesus "Lord" or "Son" conveyed a sense of the nearness of God's reign by virtue of Jesus' intimacy with the "Father" and his revelation of the nature of God. For the most part in this early stage, the word "God" was usually reserved for the Father as the creator. However, in the gospel of John the language of "Father" and "Son" was used to express the unique and eternal intimacy between God and Jesus. The Son was the one who revealed the Father: "I am the way, and the truth, and the life. No one comes to the Father except through me" (John 14:6). Speaking in the voice of Wisdom, with echoes of the intermediary from Proverbs, Jesus revealed the mystery and compassion of God: "All things have been handed over to me by my Father....Come to me, all you that are weary and carrying heavy burdens, and I will give you rest" (Matthew 11:27-28). All of these titles—"Wisdom," "Son," and "Lord"—conveyed the belief of the early community that Jesus shared in the divine nature of God.

Although Jesus revealed God through his unique intimacy with the Father, the New Testament literature also described him as a somehow distinct or separate agent of God's work. "Why do you call me good?" he asked the rich ruler in Luke's gospel. "No one is good but God alone" (Luke 18:19). To a certain degree this hierarchy was a natural one between a father and a son, or between God and his agent: "And this is eternal life, that they may know you, the only true God, and Jesus Christ whom you have sent" (John 17:3). In later centuries these hierarchical texts gave rise to conflicts, as theologians attempted to blend together the different voices of scripture into distinct doctrines of the Incarnation and the Trinity.

New Testament language about the Spirit as divine was equally rich and complex. Usually the Spirit reflected the continuing work of God in the world: "When the Advocate comes, whom I will send to you from the Father, the Spirit of truth who comes from the Father, he will testify on my behalf" (John 15:26). Received through baptism, the Spirit was the source of new life for Christians and the giver of spiritual gifts such as prophecy, healing, and discernment. The Spirit was also the inner leaven of prayer and the intimate presence of God within the believer: "Likewise the Spirit helps us in our weakness; for we do not know how to pray as we ought, but that very Spirit intercedes with sighs too deep for words" (Romans 8:26). Some early authors used twofold formulas about the Father and the Son—"Grace to you and peace from God the Father and the Lord Jesus Christ" (Galatians 1:3)—while others used threefold: "There is one body and one Spirit,...one Lord, one faith, one baptism, one God and Father of all" (Ephesians 4:4-6). From these texts and from the experiences of the early Christian communities emerged a pattern of God as triad: Father, Son and Holy Spirit. The clearest doctrinal expressions of this pattern in the New Testament probably reflect formulas that were used in worship, such as Matthew's great commission: "Go therefore and make disciples of all nations, baptizing them in the name of the Father and of the Son and of the Holy Spirit" (28:19).

As a collection of letters, hymns, and stories, the New Testament offers a rich mixture of testimonies to

Jesus. We also have other ancient works that offer additional sayings of Jesus, as well as stories and reflections about his life, but these documents were not given the same authority by the orthodox Christian community. Nevertheless, the wealth of this material helps us to understand the wide range of responses to Jesus as savior. In the New Testament the primary patterns interpret him as the Messiah who brings the reign of God and as the personification of a cosmic wisdom who has brought about a new relationship between creation and God. Later theologians would work hard to weave these images together with the developing beliefs of the early communities. The devotion and worship of Jesus at the center of community life clearly created varied interpretations of Hebrew scripture and new reflections on God.

∼ The Divine Savior

The early Christian emphasis on the power of God in Christ to embrace and transform fallen humanity was celebrated in the art, visions, and prayers of the early church. The church's theology and liturgies were deeply intertwined with images popular in the culture at the time, as Christians adapted common Hellenistic images of paradise or savior gods and gradually transformed their everyday practices of amulets, chants, and prayers to reflect their new belief in Christ.

Since the building of churches was not a common practice until the fourth century, we have only a limited number of Christian representations from this early period. The overarching theme of Christian art we do have is one of deliverance and power: images of Jonah or the good shepherd reflect not merely deliverance from death, but rebirth. As mentioned earlier, the image of Jesus as the good shepherd appeared over the baptistery in the third-century church in Dura Europas, and images of Jesus working miracles were on the side walls. At this period Jesus was usually portrayed as a youthful wonder worker, thus conveying a sense of healing power and deliverance.

Some of these themes also appear in dreams recorded by early Christians. In her diary of her martyrdom, Perpetua recorded a vision of ascending a terrible ladder of sharp weapons. Using the name of Jesus, she passed safely by a dragon—Satan—and was met in a pastoral scene by a "tall grey-haired man in shepherd's clothes." Greeting her as warmly as a child, he fed her milk and cheese. Her companion Saturus also recorded a vision of God: after their death they ascended to heaven and were greeted by an "aged man with white hair and a youthful face" who kissed them and touched their faces, directing them to "go and play."[1] These dreams of Christians enduring imprisonment and waiting for death convey a deep reassurance of divine care and paradise to come. The effect of these visions of Christ was to grant the prisoners inner peace in the midst of terror and uncertainty.

The rich intimacy of the power of Jesus may also be seen in the many images of Christ in the prayers and liturgies of the church. Baptized in the name of Christ, fed by the eucharist as the body of Christ, and bearing the name of "Christian," believers identified deeply with an interior sense of the presence of God. Ignatius described himself as a "Godbearer" and spoke of Jesus as his "inseparable life." His meditations on his approaching martyrdom reveal an intense imitation of Christ; he spoke of listening to the "silence" of Jesus and feeling his suffering as birth pangs: "My love has been crucified, and there is in me no fire of love for material things, but only living water speaking in me, saying from within, 'Come to the Father.'"[2] In a similar way, the African mother Felicitas spoke of Jesus as her interior strength in the face of approaching torture: "Another shall be inside me who will suffer for me just as I am suffering for him."[3] A prophet from Asia Minor reported a vision of Jesus as Wisdom: "Christ came to me in the likeness of a woman, clad in a bright robe, and He planted wisdom in me and revealed that this place is holy, and that here Jerusalem comes down from heaven."[4] The theologian Origen experienced Jesus as his interior guide in his meditation on scripture; the Word as teacher led each Christian individually into a deeper union with God through careful and creative reflection on the words of scripture. Origen described the many names of Jesus in scripture as reflecting levels and seasons of Christian devotion: Light, Life, Bread, Shepherd, Word. Clearly, for many early Christians Jesus was the gateway into a deeper understanding and life at the heart of reality.

Devotion to Jesus in the earliest centuries also included an affirmation of his power to save. Paul's assertion that "at the name of Jesus every knee shall bow" (Philippians 2:9) and Peter's witness that salvation is offered "by the name of Jesus Christ of Nazareth" (Acts 4:10) reveal the sense of power and identity early Christians found in the name itself. To speak of Jesus as "the name of God" referred back to speculations on the hidden name of God in the Hebrew scriptures, a name so holy that it could not be said aloud. The name of Jesus had the power to heal and to save because it revealed the transcendent and most powerful God. Egyptian Christian manuscripts from the early centuries indicate that the "sacred names"— those names written with particular reverence—were God, Lord, Jesus, and Christ. To invoke the name of Jesus or to use the sign of the cross was to call upon a divine power that was both accessible and able to intercede. Early magical papyri reveal the "Christianization" of charms by the fourth century, showing the rise of widespread belief in the efficacy of Christian power.

The richness and multiplicity of the images of the divine reflect the wondrous accessibility of God's presence and power for early Christians through Jesus as the incarnate Word and Son of God. A traditional hymn of evening we know as the *Phos hilaron* in Evening Prayer most likely dates from this period, celebrating renewal and power:

> Joyous Light of heavenly glory
> Of the immortal heavenly Father
> Holy, Blessed
> Jesus Christ,
> As the sun goes down
> And we see the evening light
> We sing a hymn to God—Father, Son,
> And Holy Spirit.
> You are always worthy
> To be sung by auspicious voices
> Son of God, Giver of life.
> That is why the world glorifies you.[5]

∿ The Suffering God

Early Christian devotion to Jesus as exclusive savior created problems with regard to both the traditional monotheism of Judaism and the polytheism of the surrounding culture. Early Roman reports of Christianity were not surprised at the claims of divinity of Jesus; wise men were assumed to achieve a semi-divine status. However, the Christian insistence on the exclusive worship of a Jesus who suffered as God violated the cultural norms of polytheism and transcendence. As Celsus, a philosophical critic of the time, put it:

> If these men worshipped no other God but one, perhaps they would have had a valid argument against others. But in fact they worship to an extravagant degree this man who appeared only recently, and yet think it is not inconsistent with monotheism.[6]

Living in a culture in which the Roman philosophical understandings of God were taken for granted and emerging from a Jewish tradition of monotheism, Christians were challenged to explain and defend their belief in a suffering divine savior.

In the second century Christians offered a number of ways to understand the divine work and status of Jesus without violating monotheism. Some Christians argued that Jesus was a prophet upon whom the Spirit descended. He should not be identified with God himself, but rather was an inspired man. This theological position was called "adoptionism," meaning that God had "adopted" Jesus as his "son" but they did not share a common divine nature, which would have compromised traditional monotheism. According to these Christians, Jesus was merely a uniquely inspired man who became the Son of God by fulfilling the will of his Father. Although the work of Jesus was decisive, his nature was not divine. Traditional monotheism was maintained and Jesus was defined as a prophet who truly suffered and was raised by God.

On the other hand, some Christians so totally identified Jesus with God that no distinction remained between the Father and the Son. Several examples of this theology were taught in Rome. One bishop named Zephyrinus said, "I know one God, Jesus Christ; nor except him do I know any other that is begotten and susceptible to suffering."[7] This position was called "modalism": God as one nature acted under different names or modes during salvation history, but did not have three distinct persons. One way to understand this theological model is to think of ourselves as one person in three different roles: for example, I am a professor, a mother, and a priest, but I am always myself, simply performing different functions. Modalism clearly affirmed the divinity of Jesus, and appeared to be a helpful way of preserving divine unity. Yet ancient theologians rejected modalism because scripture revealed God as separate persons: "We too know in truth one God; we know Christ; we know the Son suffered...and is at the right hand of the Father."[8]

In reading scripture and using the trinitarian formula in worship, orthodox Christians therefore acknowledged distinct names and persons of God even as they sought ways to state their belief that God is one. The Father was creator, while the Son became incarnate and suffered. So to identify Jesus as a "mode" or role of God violated the clear scriptural distinction between the Father and the Son as well as the actions that were distinctive to particular members of the Trinity. The church therefore rejected both adoptionism and modalism because both were inadequate in light of the scriptural evidence regarding the unique relationship of Father and Son and the divine saving role of Jesus.

Some theologians in the second century turned to the wisdom tradition of the Old Testament and Greek philosophical traditions in order to explain Jesus as the divine mediator between God and the world. By describing Jesus' eternal pre-existence with God as Word or Wisdom, they were able to borrow and transform a common cultural construction taught by later developments in the philosophy of Plato. According to Middle Platonism, a second, active aspect of divinity had been responsible for organizing the created world; some Christians who interpreted Jesus as the mediator and revealer of the transcendent Creator identified him with this aspect of divinity. Just as a human word expresses outwardly the inner thoughts of the mind, so Christ as "Word" is the will or mind of God expressed outwardly and actively into the world. Christ is therefore divine, yet distinct from the Father.

This image also affirmed the unique revelatory authority of Jesus as Wisdom or reason incarnate, revealing the inner truths of God. We see Jesus as the Word in the prologue to John's gospel, which describes the presence of the Word with God in the beginning and later in the flesh with humanity: "And the Word became flesh and lived among us, and we have seen his glory, the glory as of a father's only son, full of grace and truth" (John 1:14). For educated Christians, Jesus as the incarnate Word could sum up all the teachings of the philosophers. In his teachings, for example, Justin created a compelling argument for the universality of Christianity by identifying Jesus, the Word incarnate, with the Greek philosophical "Word" that gave all reason and order to reality. According to Justin, if the Word of the universe is the source of all human wisdom, then in following Jesus, the incarnate Word of God, Christians have become the heirs of all truth; Moses, Socrates, and the least educated of the baptized have all been taught by the same source. He therefore claimed:

> Whatever things were rightly said among all teachers are the property of us Christians. For next to God, we worship and love the Word who is from the Unbegotten and Ineffable God, since he also became man for our sakes, that becoming a partaker of our sufferings, he might also bring us healing.[9]

Justin thus offered a way of understanding Jesus as the human presence of the universal principle of order and truth so long sought by philosophers. His argument not only tried to make Christianity intelligible to Greek culture, but it also offered a way of interpreting Greek culture as a preparation for the truth of Christianity. Christianity was not just a new movement, but the fulfillment of ancient desires for truth. Justin's use of philosophy was a way of reaching out to more educated people, yet his insistence on the suffering of Christ anchored his cosmic universalism in history and common experience.

The rich philosophical images of Christ as the Word offered ways to understand the unity of the Godhead as well. In North Africa the philosopher and teacher Tertullian drew on contemporary Stoicism and Platonism to argue that Christian monotheism was only the continuation of philosophical cosmology:

> God too is spirit. When a ray is projected from the sun, it is a portion of the whole, but the sun will be in the ray, because it is the sun's ray, nor is it a division of substance, but an extension Spirit from Spirit, God from God—as light is lit from light.[10]

Another philosophical Christian, Origen in Alexandria, also used philosophy to show the hierarchy of the Trinity. As the creator of all that exists, the Father must be greater than the Son; as generated last, the Spirit must be of lesser power. This being said, Origen went on to argue that they share the same divine nature and are eternally in relation. The Son is therefore the image of the transcendent Father, the active principle of love and enlightenment toward the fallen world. The Spirit is continuously active as the means of sanctification. In this way the categories of Platonism were transformed to show the unity of the Trinity as well as the saving process of creation, incarnation, and sanctification, or new life in the Spirit.

However, when placed within this philosophical context, the biblical accounts of the suffering of Jesus became problematic. In response some Christians defended the necessity and reality of two natures in Jesus—human and divine. The incarnate word had both the power of divine nature and the vulnerability of human nature. Irenaeus put it this way:

> It was impossible that the very humanity which had once been conquered and shattered by its disobedience should reconstitute itself and obtain the prize....Therefore the Son accomplished both things. Existing as God's Word, he descended from the Father and became enfleshed and humbled himself to the point of death and completed God's program for our salvation.[11]

Because human nature had been crippled by the fall of Adam and was unable to save itself, a divine savior was necessary for salvation. However, the very humility of God in taking on human flesh to achieve salvation revealed a new order at the heart of the universe:

> The Word of God, powerful in every way,...acted justly even in opposing that same apostate power. He redeemed his own from it, not by violence, which is the way that power got control of us to begin with,...but by persuasion, for that is the proper way for a God who persuades and does not compel in order to get what he wants.[12]

The saving action of Christ was multifaceted: it was both the revelation of God's truth to all, and the transformation of human material weakness into divine immortality. Through the incarnation came participation in God, or divinization, which restored the lost image of humanity and shared the qualities of divine life. The two natures of Christ therefore reflected the fullness of the redemptive process: Christ was the Second Adam whose obedience was a model for human virtue as well as the incarnate Word who shattered the power of death and infused humanity with divine power.

Other Christians, however, approached the problem of redemption differently. Marcion wished to reject the violence of God in the Hebrew scripture, and taught that Jesus only "appeared" to be human (in Greek *dokew*, hence the term "docetism" is often used to describe this perspective) in order to reveal a new and hidden god, the Father. Like some teachers of Gnosticism, Marcion could then focus on the spiritual power of Jesus, his human nature being less important. In response, Tertullian defended physical existence as a gift from God and therefore proper to Christ: "Christ loved that human being....If Christ belongs to the Creator, then it is his own creation he loved."[13]

To defend the birth of Christ or his suffering was ultimately to assert the value of human physical existence as a necessary part of the process of salvation. An early homily said explicitly: "If Christ, the Lord who saved us, though he was originally spirit, became flesh and so called us, so also we shall receive our reward in this flesh."[14] Since material being was considered a lower state of existence in late antiquity, many systems of salvation merely discarded historical or physical life. By contrast, Christians in line with the Jewish tradition defended the goodness of physical life and defined salvation itself as the transformation of that life by union with God.

∿ The Nicene Controversy

These varied images and definitions of the identity and saving work of Jesus brought different church communities into sustained conflict in the early fourth century in what became known as the Arian or Nicene controversy. Disagreements over the precise language defining the relationship between the Father and the Son led to a series of church councils and the development of a number of creeds, as church leaders attempted to make lasting theological statements for the whole church. This fierce controversy was fueled by a number of factors, including the emperor Constantine's desire for a united church, theological and ecclesiastical rivalries between bishops, and the difficulty of the problem itself: what language is proper to speak of the eternal relationship between the Father, Son, and Holy Spirit? If we cannot speak of it, can we be sure of our salvation?

The Nicene controversy began locally in a theological argument between a bishop and a priest. In 318 Alexander, the bishop of Alexandria, was challenged by one of his priests concerning his explanation of the Trinity. Arius, a man noted for his learning and popular preaching, accused his bishop of being a modalist who did not observe the proper distinctions between the Father and the Son. Arius offered the view that if the Father was indeed the first principle and creator of all being, logically the Son as "begun" or "begotten" could not share the divine nature with the Father. Arius claimed that at one time the Son did not exist, since only the Father as the first cause of all being was "unbegun" by nature. Since the Son was created, inside or outside of time, he had to have a different nature; two beings could not be "unbegun" and share the same divinity. In his defense, Alexander declared that Arius was an adoptionist: by making the Son of a different nature or a creature, he was denying Jesus' divinity and therefore the possibility of human salvation.

The church in Alexandria became deeply divided over these theological arguments, with the clergy separating into factions and the women ascetics and laity also taking sides in the conflict. When violence and dissension continued between Christians on the streets of the city, both parties appealed for support beyond the diocese by writing letters to other bishops. Arius was condemned by a local synod, but appealed to powerful friends beyond Alexandria. This theological controversy was no longer a local affair, but had exploded throughout the wider church, east and west. The problems raised by Arius' teachings became the major theological controversy of the fourth century, and it would only be settled at the Council of Constantinople in 381 by the emperor Theodosius after sixty years of debate.

Why were the questions Arius raised so important? Clearly, the authority of bishops and the peace of the empire were at stake, but the fundamental passions appear to be theological. Since theological language about Jesus is language about salvation and hope, the images one chooses to describe the person and work of Christ are deeply tied to one's fears and convictions about life and death. For ancient Christians the relation of Jesus to the Father was the critical link to the reality of the incarnation and the eventual divinization of humanity. To argue about "Sonship" was to argue about salvation. On the other hand, if the bishops, emperors, monks, laity, and intellectuals involved shared a desire to preserve their belief in salvation, they were deeply divided as to what scriptural terms or philosophical concepts might best convey this mystery of faith and bring unity to the church.

Disturbed by dissension and violence within his new religion, Constantine called a church council in 325 to settle the matter. Although the bishops journeyed to the pleasant lakeside town of Nicaea at imperial expense for the summer and were flattered by the presence of Constantine himself in their theological debates, consensus proved hard to find. Most of the traditional scriptural language that defined the relationship of Father and Son was not precise enough to exclude the teaching of Arius. The majority of the bishops at that time were content with the old hierarchical model, which seemed to offer a unity of nature as well as a distinction between Father and Son. However, Arius' insistence on the uniqueness of the Father's nature as "unbegun" and the Son as "created" offered them little middle ground.

Finally, the council decided on a credal formula in an attempt to settle the conflict. The creed was probably an adaptation of a local baptismal creed that was modified to define the relation of the Father and the Son, including the addition of the phrase "Light from Light, true God from true God, begotten, not made" to describe the Son. The crux of the statement was a new and controversial word: *homoousios*, or "same being." A number of bishops and other Christians from the eastern church disliked the unfamiliar term; compared to traditional biblical language, it seemed to be philosophical jargon that excluded Arianism but meant little to them. They signed the creed, but set about overturning its theology.

After the council ended, those who supported the theology of the creed tried to explain the term *homoousios* and to argue for the continuing authority of the council itself for the entire church, east and west. Despite their efforts, however, the Nicene council did not immediately achieve theological consensus in the imperial church. The next five decades were marked by bitter theological debates, physical violence, repeated exiles, and a series of councils, each attempting to put forward another creed that would be accepted by the church. What we call the Nicene Creed in *The Book of Common Prayer* is in fact the later creed of the Council of Constantinople in 381, which confirmed the theology of Nicaea but added language concerning the divinity of the Holy Spirit.

Theologically, the issues at stake between Alexander and Arius emerged from continuing problems concerning monotheism. How can God be one and divided? Is the Son equal to the Father or somehow less? Because most of Arius' writings were destroyed as heretical, it is difficult for us to reconstruct his teaching with certainty. Later Arians who continued to oppose Nicaea in the fourth century did not necessarily follow his original teaching. It does appear that Arius challenged the earlier hierarchical model of Origen and Justin, which allowed a unity of nature between the Father and the Son, even if they were clearly unequal. Arius declared that the Father's nature could not be shared without compromising his unique being as the first, unbegotten principle. The

Son, who was begotten, had a beginning, and therefore must be of another nature. The Son could be
divine in some sense as the product of God, but did not
share the same divine nature as the Father.

Some scholars believe that Arius taught this sharp
distinction of natures so that he could speak directly
of the suffering and obedience of the Son. If the Son
was of a separate divine nature, Arius could speak
realistically of divine suffering and of the obedience of
the incarnate Christ without seeming to say that the
Father suffered as well. Other scholars believe Arius
was primarily defending a philosophical monotheism
that protected God from suffering or change, thus
radically distinguishing the Son from the Father. As we
discussed above, many Christians at this time felt that
the divine Word in the incarnate Christ should not be
identified with the human suffering and death of Jesus.

The response to Arius was put most forcefully not
by Alexander, but by his young successor as the bishop of Alexandria, Athanasius. Drawing upon the
teaching of Origen, Athanasius defended the eternal
generation of the Son from the Father. Because the
Father and Son were divine, as revealed in scripture,
they must by definition share the same nature and
they must have an eternal relation. Fathers and sons
share a common nature; creators and creatures do
not. Reflecting a sharper division between God and the
world than his predecessors Justin or Origen,
Athanasius argued that there could be no "secondary"
divinity; the Son either shared divine nature or was a
creature. Even more important, salvation could not be
accomplished unless Jesus was indeed God incarnate.
Without the real presence of God in Jesus, human par-

ticipation in eternal life would be impossible. Only the presence of divine nature would be effective against the ravages of death upon human nature:

The purpose of this...is that we may no longer return to earth because mere earth is what we are, but may be carried by him into the heavens because we are joined to the Logos who comes from heaven.[15]

Looking back at this controversy, we can see that these theologians were not only on new ground, but also working in a public and highly charged atmosphere. Christians had affirmed the divinity of Christ as the basis of salvation, yet finding a satisfactory theological definition of this belief proved to be extremely difficult. Scriptural language was not precise enough to address causality, and philosophical language was suspect. As we shall see in the next chapter, it took another generation with a new understanding of the Trinity to resolve the problems.

～ Conclusions

Theological reflection on the nature and work of Jesus in the first three centuries was grounded in the transition of the Christian communities from a Jewish sect to an imperial church. In the first generations Christians in a context of persecution and polytheism developed a rich theology of incarnation to explain the decisive role of Jesus in the revelation of God and the transformation of human nature: God became human so that humans might become divine. Common cosmological images of Word and Wisdom were important tools for translating the saving work of Jesus for

Hellenistic culture. These powerful images echoed Hebrew scripture and Greek philosophy while giving Jesus a unique and universal role. Yet such images presented their own theological problems which came to a head in the Arian controversy. In the end the divinity of Christ was affirmed in the pre-existence of Jesus with the Father as the Word or Son, yet the arguments around Nicaea continued as many Christians held opposing definitions of what this divinity meant. Christians confessed God as one, Father, Son, and Holy Spirit, yet did not have the technical vocabulary needed to explain this unity or to resolve differences about such teachings.

This multiplicity of images and teachers reflects the creativity and deep faith of the first three centuries. Until the fourth century, the geographically scattered Christian communities simply separated over irreconcilable differences. When Origen disagreed with his bishop in Alexandria, he moved to be with friendlier bishops in Caesarea and never returned to Alexandria. In the fourth century, however, theological problems had to be resolved in the context of public debate because the church was now a public institution funded by the emperor. Bishops had to balance their loyalty to local traditions as well as negotiate with the larger church as they began to attend councils. The intense theological conflicts of the fourth and fifth centuries show not only the intellectual development of Christianity, but also how Christians who were now prominent under imperial patronage needed to find ways to live together as followers of Jesus.

Chapter Seven

Who is God?

Credal Orthodoxy from Nicaea to Chalcedon

The fourth and fifth centuries are the age of the great theological debates over the Christian doctrines of the Trinity and the Incarnation—debates about the nature of Jesus and his relationship to the Father and the Spirit. The conclusions of these bitter and often violent conflicts are recorded in the creeds we say today and form the basis of the church's beliefs. The history of formulating these doctrines calls us to understand that theology is always a human task, and therefore reflects all the flaws and glories of our human nature. In the ancient church theology was written not by academics in university libraries or bishops in private session. Instead, reflecting the vigorous urban life of the time, the whole church was often involved through the writings of bishops, the debates of theologians, the rallies of believers, and the interventions of monks. These divisions over central beliefs were passionately opposed or defended by everyone because they appeared to threaten salvation itself. Equally important, tradition was increasingly codified through written creeds. These documents were carefully worded theological compromises, yet as written and somehow frozen, they became the means to test and limit theological pluralism.

The work of theology in this era was truly "political"—it was the work of the *polis*, the whole city. Alliance and negotiation were essential to the creation of consensus in a divided and passionate community. Obviously, some members by education and office had more power than others, yet at this time through regular hearing of preaching, private reading, and oral debate ordinary people had deeply held theological positions as well. Ironically, the centripetal force of imperial politics that drew bishops together to build theological consensus often uncovered and even increased conflicts between the different traditions of their local churches. Orthodoxy readily became a tool of power politics as bishops competed with one another for the prestige and privileges of their diocese and city. Yet by the same token power was not the only motivation, and many Christians suffered exile and abuse in defense of teaching they believed was true.

In the last chapter we looked at the development of the church's understanding of Jesus and the early attempts to describe his incarnate life. In this chapter we will see how the credal definitions of the church about God as Trinity emerged from these intensely political and profoundly theological debates of the fourth and fifth centuries. Lasting consensus was only achieved after years of discussion, and sometimes it was never achieved. In the eastern church the Arian crisis was resolved only after a dozen councils met during the years between Nicaea (325) and Constantinople (381). Questions concerning the doctrine of the Incarnation divided the eastern church again at Ephesus in 431, and these were barely settled at the council of Chalcedon in 451. Indeed, these christological issues continue to divide the Eastern Orthodox tradition in our present day.

Why should Christians argue over theology? In religious life faith is primary because it reflects our deepest beliefs and commitments. Theology is the secondary reflection on that faith, yet its language and images either limit or broaden our understanding and experience of God. Theology is therefore critical to the life and vitality of a faith community. In divided communities—like those of the fourth and fifth centuries—theology is a language not only about God, but about our deepest hopes and fears. It is the articulation of our inheritance and saving tradition that cannot be changed easily. However, living theology and faith must eventually move beyond intellectual debate or inherited tradition into the shared spiritual task of prayer, negotiation, and compromise in light of the ultimate mystery of God.

～ Theologies of the Trinity

Although the council of bishops at Nicaea signed a creed that condemned the teachings of Arius and supported those of Bishop Alexander of Alexandria, the wording of the formula of one substance or being, *homoousios*, proved to be difficult for many to accept. The majority of Christians held the view of a common divinity between the Father and Son, rejecting Arius' extreme view of the Son as "created," but they were reluctant to use the non-biblical language to express this truth. The traditional hierarchical model giving superior status to the Father as creator continued to dominate. Over the following decades a series of councils attempted to find a formula to replace the troublesome language of Nicaea and bring consensus to the east, but these efforts were complicated by ecclesiastical rivalries, changes in emperors, and the sheer complexities of the doctrine of the Trinity. Like many present-day bishops, these bishops were reluctant to discuss controversial choices in a public arena; they would rather not make a choice between Athanasius' new creed or Arius' controversial teaching.

The basic objection to the original Nicene creed was a fear of obscuring the distinction between Father and Son, and therefore falling into an unscriptural modalism. *Homoousios* seemed to blur the separate identities of the Father and Son. At this early stage of theological discussion the problem was in part linguistic. Theological language was not being used consistently within the east itself, much less between the Greek of the east and the Latin of the west. For some the Greek word *hypostasis* could mean "nature" and refer to *one* single nature of God; God as Father, Son, and Holy Spirit had one *hypostasis*. In complete contradiction, others held it meant a particular existence or "person," so the Trinity was made of *three* separate individuals or *hypostases*. Wishing to avoid these confusing philosophical terms altogether, many conservative theologians in the years following Nicaea searched for a formula based solely on biblical language. Thus, in 341 the council of Antioch declared the Son to be "only-begotten" and "co-existent with the Father" by using such biblical words about God as wisdom, way, truth, will, and glory. Athanasius and his followers rejected this formula: to them *homoousios* was the only definition of God that guaranteed the Son shared fully in the divine nature and could thus enable us to share in the new life of God through the taking on of human nature.

Emperors were discouraged by the ongoing fighting within the church, and continued to call councils in hopes of bringing peace. The successful general Constantius, a son of Constantine who succeeded his father, sought to suppress paganism and build unity in the church by enforcing a new creed from Sirmium in 356. This formula stated clearly that the Son was subordinate to the Father and banned the use of any "substance" language that could ascribe a common nature to the Father and Son. The Nicene party labeled the creed a "blasphemy" and the emperor the "Antichrist." Other theological positions were likewise put forward in an attempt to find a binding creed. Basil of Ancyra, for example, offered a compromise of "like" substance: his term was *homoiousios*, leading historians to claim the church was divided over one iota!

Equally important, problems of innovation and tradition perplexed many. Some who were able to accept the shared nature of Father and Son challenged the divinity of the Spirit: was it not "created" with all things by the Word, as set out in the prologue of John's gospel? The complexities of the language and the range of exegesis reveal the diversity of interpretations existing in the communities at the time. If bound together by a common faith in salvation through Christ, they were divided by different theological traditions.

This theological confusion was intensified by the unlikely ascension of a pagan emperor, Julian, to the throne in 360. Eager to restore the glories of Rome through a return to the traditional worship of the gods, Julian allowed all dissenting Christian parties an equal hearing and brought them home from exile. Popular violence among dissenting Christians and between pagans and Christians increased, as all levels of the population argued over urgent questions of salvation: How can we be saved if Jesus was not fully divine? How can we read scripture and not accept that a son is less than a father? Gregory of Nyssa resented these popular discussions of theology:

> If you ask anyone for change, he will discuss with you whether the Son is begotten or unbegotten. If you ask about the quality of bread, you will receive an answer, "The Father is greater, the Son is less."[1]

Bishops were increasingly vulnerable because they were accountable to local people as representatives of their doctrinal beliefs at the imperial councils. One bishop mumbled during critical points of prayer to avoid taking sides: the Arians prayed *to* the Father, *through* the Son, and *in* the Holy Spirit, while the Nicenes prayed to *all* persons of the Trinity.

With the controversy dragging on, Athanasius called a council in Alexandria in 362 to sort out some of the linguistic difficulties and find common ground among the opposing parties. Recognizing the essential

necessity of trinitarian faith, however flawed in ter-
minology, the council affirmed that those who spoke
of one *hypostasis* were in agreement with those who
spoke of three; the Trinity could be understood as having three persons in one nature. Athanasius himself
had been reluctant to use *homoousios* extensively, and
instead had argued for the acceptance of Nicaea based
on the eternal unity of the Father and the Son as consistently revealed in scripture. For God and Jesus to be
called in scripture Father and Son, they had to share
the same eternal divinity: "In the case of deity alone,
the Father is properly father and the Son is properly
son, and for them and them alone is it that the Father
is always father and the Son is always son."[2] The
names of God therefore had to be interpreted in accordance with the qualities of divine nature: eternal and
changeless. "Because God is, he is everlasting; and
because the Father always is, his reflection, which is
his Word, is also everlasting."[3] To confess the Son as
God must mean that his nature is identical to the
divinity of the Father. This ensured the integrity of
the revelation of scripture as well as the possibility
of a human being becoming divine through the
incarnation.

∼ The Cappadocians
The architects of theological unity in the east were
three bishops known as the Cappadocians: two brothers, Basil of Caesarea and Gregory of Nyssa, and
Basil's friend, Gregory Nazianzus. Known by the
name of their homeland in central Turkey,
Cappadocia, these ascetic bishops came from distinguished Christian families and were well-educated,

with a keen interest in theology and spirituality. Basil had initially been hesitant to accept the concept of *homoousios*, but after the compromise of Alexandria in 362 he worked out an understanding of the Trinity as one nature *(ousia)* in three modes of existence or persons *(hypostasis)*, thus ensuring the unity and distinction of the Godhead. Pressed concerning his beliefs about the divinity of the Spirit, he argued on the basis of liturgical practice for the unity of the Trinity because of the lack of clear scriptural evidence. The specific theology of the Holy Spirit may have been passed over in silence by earlier authors, Basil claimed, but "as we were baptized, so we believe; as we believe, so also we give praise:...we glorify the Holy Spirit together with the Father and Son."[4]

Steeped in the dynamic spirituality of Origen and contemporary asceticism, the Cappadocians wrote extensively on theology and spirituality. They believed that tradition unfolds over time, and that God alone could reveal divine mysteries. Because the divine nature is transcendent and beyond human intellect, it follows that we may speak of theology only in the terms given to us by God.

> Following the suggestions of scripture, we have learned that the divine nature is unnameable and unutterable. We say that every name, whether it has been invented from human usage or handed down from scripture, is an interpretation of things thought about divine nature and does not encompass the significance of divine nature itself.[5]

According to the Cappadocians, the Arians were wrong to base their arguments only on the definition of God as creator or father, for these were only human interpretations of an unknown and eternal mystery. We must accept the revelation of God as "Father" and "Son" rather than apply principles of causality to the divine mystery. Thus, the distinct "persons" of the Godhead must each be eternal, given the transcendent unity of god: God is always Father, Son, and Holy Spirit. Given the unity of divine nature, the whole Trinity therefore works in each action of God. Spiritual progress is growth in our knowledge of God, but because God is infinite, our exploration of mystery is also delightfully infinite. Love will never end. Created in the image of God, our contemplation of the Trinity increases our joy and intimacy, ultimately transforming us into friends of God.

The work of the Cappadocians laid the foundation for theological consensus in the east. The emperor Theodosius called a council to meet in Constantinople in 381, with the understanding that it would support Nicene orthodoxy. The eternal sonship of Christ and the term *homoousios* were affirmed. In contrast to the earlier creed at Nicaea, the Constantinople council added a long section on the divinity of the Spirit, using a combination of biblical phrases and testimonies to the actions of the Spirit. This is the creed we say today in our liturgies as the Nicene creed (BCP 358). The original wording in 381 concerning the procession of the Spirit was "from the Father." However, western Christians later changed this phrase to "from the Father and Son" as a defense against Arianism's interpretation of the Son as a lesser being. In Latin this phrase is *filioque*, and to this day it is cited by the eastern church as an illegitimate change in the written creed. Theodosius exiled radical Arians in an effort to enforce the creed, and for the most part this creed achieved the unity that had been sought for so long.

With its complex theological and political history, the construction of trinitarian orthodoxy in the fourth century fosters many interpretations. To some theologians, credal orthodoxy is the way the state imposed unity and order on the complexity and diversity of early Christianity. For others it is the story of a valiant Nicene party fighting heretical Arian emperors and conspirators to keep the truth alive. It certainly involved the negotiation of power, theological uncertainty, loyalty to tradition, and openness to innovation within a unified, if quarreling, community.

As we have seen, the formula at Nicaea that was adopted to exclude Arius only began the argument, and the theological debate of the church soon moved beyond it. Clearly, ecclesiastical rivalries interfered with consensus as much as authentic theological difference. Yet the doctrine of salvation, the authority of scripture, and a new understanding of God as Trinity were at stake in these debates. The passion for the defense of the reality of salvation through Christ encouraged popular participation. Emperors such as Constantius or Theodosius had clear theological preferences, but without a growing consensus in the church their councils would be unenforceable. Imperial orthodoxy was therefore deeply political in the sense of being a public and negotiated formula,

but it was also deeply theological. The painfully craft-
ed language of the creeds protected the scriptural
inheritance as well as the developing spirituality of
incarnation.

~ Theologies of Incarnation

If Nicene orthodoxy defended the full divinity of
Christ, problems still existed as to how this essential
Word of God could take on human flesh and die. One
of the most brilliant defenders of Nicene orthodoxy
was Apollinarius of Laodicea, a friend of Athanasius
and an advisor to Basil. Together with his father, he
was a teacher of classics as well as Christianity.
Disturbed by the Arian attack on the essential divinity of the Son, Apollinarius wrote extensively about
the necessity of God becoming flesh in order to achieve
salvation. Seeking to teach how we may understand
the Nicene affirmation of the divine Son incarnate, he
explored a number of theological options. He taught
that in Christ the Word took the place of the human
mind or soul in a man. This solution maintained that
Jesus had a true, bodily fleshly existence, but that the
divine Logos was the source of all activity or will. He
could therefore speak of "one" nature in Christ.

The response to his theological teaching was immediately critical. Rather than defending human participation in divinity, his opponents argued, Apollinarius
was in fact undercutting divinization by denying the
presence of a full and therefore real humanity in the
incarnation: if the Word did not take on our complete humanity, then he cannot redeem us. Gregory
Nazianzus defended the earlier idea that only a fully
human and fully divine Christ could save us.

Otherwise, he wrote, "how does this touch me? For Godhead joined to flesh alone is not man, nor to soul alone, nor to both apart from intellect, which is the most essential part of humanity."[6] A fully human intellect needed to be joined to the Word as well as the body in order for healing and transformation to take place. The work of salvation offered by Apollinarius was incomplete.

Yet how could the church talk about Christ being both divine and human? As we have seen, ancient theologians were reluctant to attribute Jesus' suffering to his divine nature; fear or pain was part of his human experience as revealed in scripture, but not proper to the divine nature. Over the next decades the responses to Apollinarian and Arian teaching revealed two main schools of thought in the eastern church about the incarnation. In Alexandria, where Athanasius lived and worked, theologians focused on the divine Word as the subject of salvific action, and spoke directly of his birth, suffering, and death. The attributes of divine nature—that is, qualities of impassibility and eternity—were in the incarnation mysteriously communicated to human nature in order to give us immortality. Human nature itself tended to be seen as passive in this theology, needing divine power and presence in order to heal and restore its blurred and fallen image of God. Because the focus was on the action of the Word enfleshed, Alexandrians used paradoxical statements such as the "blood of God" to affirm the wonder of God taking flesh.

In Antioch, however, a different picture emerged. There they read scripture in a way that affirmed both the operation of divine will in sacred history and the importance of human free will. The Antiochenes taught the incarnation as a union of two natures in Jesus, divine and human, emphasizing the full participation of both natures while distinguishing them sharply. Divine nature communicated immortality and transcendence, for example, but scriptural passages concerning suffering or fear referred to the courageous human nature of Christ. Christ was the Second Adam who modeled the human life of virtue, as well as the incarnate Son who brought an end to our alienation from God. The difficulty for the Antiochenes was to defend the unity of the person of Christ: how could the two be one?

These interpretations of the mystery of the incarnation were not necessarily opposed, but they came into open conflict in the fifth century when they were mixed with church politics. A battle broke out when Nestorius, the new bishop of Constantinople, preached against calling Mary by the popular title of "Godbearer," or *Theotokos*. As an Antiochene, he felt this title confused the proper distinctions of humanity and divinity in Christ. God, the pre-existent Son, could not be literally "born," for he has an eternal divine nature. Instead, Nestorius insisted that it was Christ, the incarnate union of divinity and humanity, who was physically born of Mary; he suggested that Christians use the term *Christokos* for Mary as more theologically precise. Nestorius could have been motivated by fears of a pagan interpretation of gods being born and dying, but *Theotokos* was a traditional and beloved title for Mary that embodied for many the paradoxical glory of God as an infant. His sermon was received with outrage.

Angry at Nestorius for interfering in his diocese on other matters, Cyril, the bishop of Alexandria, took the occasion to write letters against him, charging him with adoptionism and denying the divinity of Christ. Cyril went so far as to write about "one nature" in Christ, and ended up sounding much like Apollinarius. In this argument about Mary, we see the different emphasis of each theological tradition: the Alexandrians affirming the mystery of God humbly made flesh and the Antiochenes defending the full reality of both human and divine natures. Both taught divinization through incarnation, but sought through their own traditions to defend different insights into the same mystery.

A furious theological and political battle soon raged. Cyril put up posters in Constantinople releasing the laity from their obedience to Nestorius as a "heretical" bishop. The emperor, who was sympathetic to Nestorius, tried to mediate, but Cyril intended not only to exile his rival, but also to reinforce the higher prestige of Alexandria over Constantinople. Constantinople was the imperial capital, but since it was founded only a century earlier by Constantine, it could not truly boast of being one of the ancient apostolic sees such as Rome, Antioch, Jerusalem, or Alexandria. Just as his uncle Theophilus had humbled John Chrysostom, so the proud and powerful bishop of Alexandria acted against Nestorius.

When the emperor finally called a council at Ephesus in 431, both sides were prepared for theological and political battle. Cyril brought monks from the desert as well as various political allies, and Nestorius hired toughs from the local bath as body guards.

When the episcopal supporters of Nestorius were delayed in arriving at Ephesus, Cyril insisted on beginning the council, now full of his supporters, anyway. He was able to condemn and depose Nestorius with dispatch. The populace paraded through the streets of Ephesus in defense of the title *Theotokos*. Ironically, Ephesus was historically the site of the great temple to the goddess Artemis; in Paul's time, according to Acts 19, the people had rioted in favor of her. In spite of Nestorius' protests and the support of his bishops when they finally arrived, the emperor accepted the decision of the council as valid. Nestorius went into exile, where he wrote a long defense of his theology, including a vivid exposé of Cyril's political manipulations.

With the political interests satisfied, some of the christological issues were able to be resolved. In dialogue with John of Antioch, Cyril gave up his use of "one nature," and accepted the use of "two natures" for Christ. However, many of his followers felt betrayed by his compromise of traditional Alexandrian theology, so the controversy continued to smoulder. After Cyril's death, an extreme position was put forward by Eutyches, a monk who taught that in the incarnation Christ indeed had only one nature; his human nature was unlike ours, being totally transformed by union with the divine Son. The devotion to this position was again linked to the belief in the divinization of humanity, since the whole point of sacramental and devotional life was to become like God. In the ensuing controversy Eutyches was defended by a new bishop of Alexandria, Dioscorus, and in

449 another violent council in Ephesus denied seating to Roman delegates and declared Eutyches orthodox.

The council of Chalcedon met in 451 under a new emperor Marcian who rejected the violence and theology of 449. Showing both traditionalism and piety, this council affirmed the Nicene Creed in its final statement, and added a clause concerning the divine and human natures of Christ. Drawing on the earlier argument of Gregory Nazianzus that a complete human nature must be present in the incarnate Christ, they rejected again the one-nature formula. God as incarnate has two natures, divine and human, in one person, Jesus Christ. The formula itself drew on both Alexandrian and Antiochene language in order to embrace the insights of both theological traditions. When we contemplate Christ, we see the fullness of divine nature and the fullness of human nature: we see the face of God and we see our own face as it should become. In this one person we can contemplate the mystery of God revealed and the mystery of ourselves redeemed.

Although it had theological authority in the west, Chalcedon did not achieve lasting unity in the eastern church. In Egypt and Syria, for example, one-nature theology, or Monophysitism, was a traditional and deeply cherished belief seemingly rooted in the teaching of Athanasius and Cyril. Their bishops who signed the creed warned that they would be lynched at home for changing such a traditional teaching; some in fact were. Those who opposed the formula of Chalcedon insisted the creed of Nicaea was a sufficient test for doctrinal orthodoxy. The first use of the Nicene Creed in the eucharistic liturgy originated in this conflict, as anti-Chalcedonians sought to assert their orthodoxy based on Nicaea alone. The western church, of course, embraced Chalcedon as a definitive statement of Christology, but the issues were really eastern, rooted in the spiritual traditions of Egypt, Antioch, Syria, and Constantinople. The fierce debate, which had begun in the east, continued there long past the council of Chalcedon.

⮽ Conclusions

In his history of these centuries, the church historian Socrates noted that often in doctrinal arguments the opponents seem to be like two armies fighting a battle in the dark. Reflecting intense belief and pride in local tradition, these early Christian communities seemed unable to see opposing views or to negotiate compromises. The adversarial tone of the debates over "orthodoxy" versus "heresy" did not help bring peace. The high stakes of loyalty, alliance, imperial power, and privilege, not to mention the defense of orthodoxy, deeply complicated theological issues. In the end, the creeds are compromise documents setting boundaries on interpretation, but not presuming to settle all questions.

The Nicene and Chalcedonian controversies remain important watersheds in Christian theology. The statements that emerged are anchored in the ancient church's reading of scripture and logic of redemption. To ensure salvation of mutable flesh, Jesus must be the divine Word incarnate; this incarnation must enfold both divine and human nature. Yet, as we have seen, the language and exegesis needed to ensure consensus or at least limit debate were difficult and complex. Contemporary Hellenistic issues such as transcendence and impassibility profoundly shaped and limited both "orthodox" and "heretical" arguments. Athanasius and the Cappadocians not only used scripture, but also Platonic realism to defend the Trinity. If belief in Jesus as divine savior was traditional, theological reflection on this belief required creativity and insight. Our inheritance is found as much in the process of reflection as in the formulas.

In the fourth and fifth centuries, the real darkness surrounding these communities therefore was the theological future. Christians were struggling with questions that had no clear answers in scripture or tradition. To move beyond cherished traditions in order to address new problems as a community requires patient discernment and inevitably involves conflict. Theological uncertainties challenge both the heart and the intellect, whatever the political stakes. The lasting responses were those theologies of God that opened up the life of the spirit as well as set the boundaries of the community.

Chapter Eight

The Church in Late Antiquity

Saints and Sinners in the City of God

In 410 when the Goths decided to collect their over-
due military wages by sacking the city of Rome,
Christians and pagans alike were dismayed, wonder-
ing how divine providence had failed to protect the
ancient imperial capital. In the western Roman Empire
this event was the first of a series of invasions and
military defeats that would undermine Christian optimism about the newly arrived reign of God. As we
have seen in the chapters above, in three centuries
Christianity had been transformed from a persecuted
and secret sect to the dominant and complex religion
of the Roman state. And yet if Christians had challenged and changed the social and religious landscape
of late antiquity by their devotion to Jesus, they
themselves had also been changed. If baptism no
longer meant becoming a social outcast or changing
professions, what did sacramental rebirth in Christ

mean? If Christian ascetics seemed to live like angels in the flesh, how should everyday Christians live? If military invasions and popular violence still happened in the Christian state in spite of imperial patronage and regular public worship, who were the people of God?

∼ The Donatist Controversy

A century after Constantine, the North African congregations remained bitterly and violently divided over the question of Christian purity. In 311 a contested episcopal election had taken place in Carthage. The consecration of the new bishop was said to be invalid, since one of the participating bishops had once compromised his faith by turning over the scriptures to the Roman authorities. In North Africa such a fact made the case simple: since the time of Cyprian, the church had held that sacraments administered by sinful clergy were invalid. As a single and holy body, by definition, the church could not contain sinners. After the election, Christians in North Africa had been divided into two irreconcilable churches, despite Constantine's attempts to solve the division. Passions over safeguarding the purity of the church ran deep, and the theological debates continued in the century following. This conflict—which ended only with the intervention of imperial troops called in by Augustine in order to enforce conformity—reveals much about Christian identity in the fifth century. In this century the church faced continuing conflicts among local theologies as well as shifting ideals of Christian purity and identity in a Christianized society.

Upholding Cyprian's defense of the holiness and unity of the church, Donatus and his followers felt that sinful and unworthy leaders would compromise the spiritual validity of the whole church. The integrity of the church rested on the integrity of its members. According to the Donatists' understanding of unforgivable sins, generosity toward apostasy was in fact a compromise of baptismal vows and a pollution of the whole community. The efficacy of the sacraments was therefore dependent on the spiritual purity of the church; schismatics who wished to return to the church had to be rebaptized. The continuing struggles with their opponents only confirmed the Donatist view of the church as a place engaged in a struggle with a demonic world. They denied any special role to the emperor in the church, moreover, resisting much of the assimilation of language and culture that was happening in other areas of the empire. The huge baptisteries and churches they built to honor martyrs reflected their passionate belief in the transformation of human life as entailing a complete renunciation of the larger world.

Other North Africans, such as Augustine, rejected these views as outside the mainstream of the Roman imperial church. Baptism in the name of the Trinity was valid regardless of the moral state of the person who did it, because the power of the sacrament came directly from the Holy Spirit, not from the church. Given the realities of the human condition, the church would inevitably contain a mixture of saints and sinners, and only at the last judgment would these be sorted out by Christ himself. Unity and charity under the discipline of the church were the only means of purity in this life, and they would always be provisional. Boasts of purity inevitably led to hypocrisy, and Augustine himself could list numbers of clergy in the Donatist church who could be convicted of improper behavior.

Finally, Augustine argued, how did the Donatist church dare to claim to be the only true church in the vast empire of so many Christian churches? Could one man pollute a whole communion? To catholics such as Augustine, the Donatist focus on purity reflected the greater sin of sectarianism. Quoting their common African ancestor, Cyprian, he noted that schism was the worst sin of the community. Only the church as a whole had a right to judge those who fractured its unity. Appealing to the state for military aid, Augustine eventually supported the suppression of the Donatist movement. Although the Donatists represented the earliest ideals of sectarian Christianity, their more rigorous tradition was ultimately at odds with the imperial and catholic church of the fifth century.

∽ Christian Perfectionism

If the Donatist controversy threw questions about the purity and unity of the imperial church into high relief, the Pelagian controversy challenged the emerging elitism of the ascetic movement. When Pelagius came to Rome from England as a teacher of ascetics, he encouraged his lay followers, especially women, to hold themselves to the highest standards of virtue. Believing in the innate free will of humans, he taught that God commands each individual to observe the law and follow Jesus' teaching. This freedom was the key to moral accountability, and Pelagius fiercely rejected any sort of fatalistic teaching or election theology that might compromise our free will. Pelagius denied that nature might determine will; rather, bad habits were responsible for much social and individual evil. Basing his view of Christian society on the search for perfection rather than the practice of renunciation, he condemned the misuse of wealth and power. When he read Augustine's *Confessions*, he objected to its sense of overpowering divine purpose, which seemed to undercut the reality of moral freedom. Unless humans were responsible for their actions, they would not merit the goodness of the acts they performed. Grace completed every action, but human initiative was needed to begin a good work.

The fall of Rome sent Christian refugees through North Africa on their way to the Holy Land, and they brought Pelagius' teachings to the notice of Augustine. Weary and embittered by his controversy with the Donatists, Augustine attacked what appeared to be yet another system anchored in the arrogance of attaining human purity rather than in the mystery of divine grace and love. From his own experience Augustine believed that humans were incapable of completing their good intentions apart from divine aid. Pelagius' optimism about human perfection for all and the ability of the sacraments to illuminate the will seemed to him to be utterly naive. To Augustine, human freedom was the *problem* of salvation, not its source. After the fall of Adam, we developed a disordered vision of the self centered on pride rather than on the love of God. The church was not a school for the wise, but a hospital for sinners who would be lost and dead without the regular sacramental life. We were baptized in order to save ourselves from damnation, not for illumination.

Although Pelagius denied many of the implications drawn from his teaching, Augustine continued to attack his theology, using the occasion to reflect on the questions of divine activity and grace. Intellectually and emotionally he became increasingly convinced of the utter reliance of human beings on the mystery of divine grace. In the western church the fall of Adam had been interpreted as a physical event, with subsequent generations sharing in the fallen flesh and disordered will of the first ancestors. Given our inability to save ourselves, only the mercy of God intervened in order to save some; this mystery of election and predestination protected the primacy of God's will in salvation and also guaranteed it. Augustine went so far as to argue for a teaching of double predestination, in which God decided who would be saved and who would be damned.

In the words of one scholar, Augustine had constructed a defense of Christian mediocrity. If Pelagius proclaimed a universal call to perfection, Augustine proclaimed a universal need of grace.[1] In the imperial church baptism was no longer the entry into a community whose membership demanded high standards for the ordinary Christian. Asceticism had created hierarchies of perfection within the community. Augustine thus espoused asceticism as necessary for clerical life and authority. However, all Christians regardless of vocation were subject to the mysteries of grace and the sacraments. Purity and perfection did not define the Christian life, but need of God.

∾ Augustine of Hippo

Augustine's response to the Donatists's defense of purity and the Pelagian urge to perfection reflected not only his experience, but the emerging catholic church of the fifth century. An enduring and dominant voice in western thought well beyond the period of the early church, Augustine recorded his life and theology in a remarkable autobiography. In his *Confessions* he reflected on the nature of God as well as his own desperate search for certainty and purpose in his ambitious life. The church and imperial society formed and anchored this unique quest.

At first rejecting the passionate Christianity of his mother, Monnica, Augustine left Africa for Rome to seek fame as a rhetorician. Christianity appeared too crude for his tastes. Disappointed and restless, he moved through an early infatuation with Manichaean thought, with its dualistic overtones, into Platonism, where he encountered God as goodness and beauty. In Platonism evil was no longer the eternal opposing principle it was for the Manichees, but was instead the absence of good. Through the teachings of Christian Platonists, and especially those of his mentor, Ambrose of Milan, Augustine gradually returned to Christianity but with a deep reliance on the mysterious power and grace of God in his spiritual quest. Surrender to God was part of the transcending of his own ego and ambition: "You were there before my eyes, but I had deserted even my own self. I could not find myself, much less find you."[2] In order to pursue his new-found faith, Augustine became an ascetic and moved back to North Africa, where he was ordained and eventually became the bishop of Hippo.

Reflecting both his Platonism and his intense spiritual search, Augustine emphasized interior experience and intellectual analogy as the way to seek and find God. Platonism had taught that interior images were more dependable than external perceptions, and likewise for Augustine interior reflection became the means of understanding divine mysteries. As Rome was invaded by looting soldiers and the church was increasingly divided by controversy, the social chaos around him confirmed his belief that eternal realities were the place to fix the heart. As shown in the arguments with the Donatists or with Pelagius, Augustine turned from the church's earlier, more confident view of the church living as the redeemed here on earth. History had not been completed in the establishment of the imperial church. Rather, the church was a mixed body of sinners and saints who were on a pilgrimage through the fallen world to the last times. Augustine believed that God would assist the elect, through the mysterious power of grace, to remain faithful until the end.

Augustine's disappointment and lack of confidence in both society and the visible church is outlined most clearly in his work *The City of God*. Here Christians are pilgrims living in hope and trying to maintain a disciplined love of God. In the text two cities represent opposing ways of being: the way of God and the way of the world. The church cannot be identified with the city of God because the elect are hidden in the mysterious will of God. The social disorder of the day reflects the misery of the fallen world and mirrors the internal disorder of the individual. Only false peace and justice exist in this perversion of God's true plan;

the virtues of the ancient philosophers are in fact vices, as they were developed apart from the word of God in Christ. Holiness is therefore fully attainable only in a future reign of God; in this world it is largely invisible. Christians live forward in faithfulness and hope, but should not place their faith in any lesser reality than faith in God's saving will.

As an educated bishop, Augustine drew upon philosophy and scripture as well as his own spirituality to sort out answers to the issues pressing the church of his day. His teachings on the Trinity, for example, reflect both his affirmation of the hidden mystery and power of God to save those whom God chooses to save, as well as the reality of a deep and loving intimacy between the believer and the Holy Spirit. In one of his most creative works, *On the Trinity*, he used human mental faculties as an analogy for the Trinity: just as the single mind contains memory, reason, and will, so the one God may be understood as Father, Son, and Holy Spirit. In his writings on the Trinity Augustine also explored the nature of reciprocal love: the Trinity is reflected in the relations of the one who loves, the beloved, and the power of love between them. "Thus, these are each in themselves, but are also in one another, because the loving mind is also in love, and love is in the knowledge of the person loving and knowledge in the knowing mind."[3] Because humans are created in the image of God, these internal reflections provide the means to understand the mysterious God.

For many historians Augustine's somber vision of the church and the world marks the beginning of the medieval period in western history. The construction

of the church as a complex hierarchical institution
with the sole authority to save, with the Bible as the
main authoritative text for life, seems to confirm a
total Christian victory over the broader tides of classical civilization. Not only has sacred space and time
become Christianized through the expansion of the
churches, pilgrimage, and the Christian calendar, but
society itself is now viewed through a more literal
biblical vision. The world which gave birth to
Christianity has been altered beyond recognition, even
as the old religious titles have been incorporated into
the church: Pontifex Maximus was the title of the
emperor, and is now the title of the pope. Though
Hellenic culture will remain vital within the eastern
church for the next five hundred years, political disruption and uncertainty will be the story of the west.
Pope Gregory the Great will emerge to negotiate with
migrating tribal kings who invade Italy, while the
clergy replace the Latin government and provide stability of leadership in the west. During the lifetime of
Augustine of Hippo, late antiquity began to pass into
the new western cultures of the medieval age.

～ The People of God

The history of the church is the story of a community. Such an institutionalized pilgrimage has the poten-
tial to create humility among its members as well as
pretensions to authority. As we have seen, if divided
by extremes of wealth and rank, Christian society of
late antiquity was deeply unified through their common salvation in the body of Christ. The poor were no
longer invisible, but equal members of the body. As
the church developed beyond late antiquity, this vision

of a common salvation can be seen in the balanced monastic life of the community of Benedict, the passionate missionary activities of the Celtic monks, the pastoral papacy of Gregory the Great, and the leadership of the learned abbesses Hilda and Leoba.

Left as the only apostolic see in the west, in the early medieval period Rome will become the sole arbiter of Christian culture and the source of social stability in the west. The eastern church will appeal to Rome for confirmation or mediation on occasion, but will continue largely on its own theological path. In both east and west the heated theological debates will crystalize into written authorities who will be recovered only by scribes. The dissenting voices will become only the shadows of those ancestors who were considered orthodox, their theological perspectives reduced to formulas identified by simple labels. The rich local traditions will be submerged by invading Vandals and Muslims or fractured into Monophysites and Chaledonians. Christian institutions and missionaries will struggle to adapt this legacy to western tribal cultures.

Many have noted the close affinity of our modern world to the earlier world of late antiquity. Our technology and global politics have created another cosmopolitan world of local cultures united beneath a veneer of a common culture. Urban life has the dominant voice, though many live in traditional, rural environments. Although disproportionate economies have divided people living in the various countries of the world, global communication and the spread of democracy have made a wider variety of voices accessible. In the west global unity has awakened us again

to problems of diverse cultures and conflicting religious beliefs, especially as we continue to live with the
consequences of nineteenth-century imperialism.
When we speak we now hear our voices as only one
of many perspectives.

Unity and multiplicity are themes common to both
late antiquity and our own age. Recovering the struggles of earlier Christians is a helpful legacy when we
understand ourselves as created, provisional beings
living under a larger mystery. Their stubborn provin-
cialism, their astute political insights, and their theological passions have much to teach us as we struggle
with the effects of nationalism and religious misun-
derstandings today. In some ways they are ahead of
us: schooled in the rhetorical arts, they knew how to
find and build consensus. Sobered by the costs of
Christian baptism and martyrdom, they held salvation dear. The language of unity and authority
assumed a lively lay participation as much as it relied
on certain assumptions of gender and class. As
revealed in the continuing leadership of women from
the apostles to the ascetics, the charismatic realities
of the gospel continued to be held in tension with
social conformity. Acknowledging the local traditions
of Africa, Alexandria, Rome, and Constantinople, the
early Christians expected a unity born out of diversity and discernment.

As we Anglicans seek to understand our role in the
twentieth-first century, we need to remember these
first struggles over unity and plurality. The union of
diverse and sometimes conflicting traditions into a
reformed catholicity was the vision of the original
English reformers. In our desire for unity or in our

nostalgia for the past, we may forget that theological diversity is also part of an apostolic church. Although theological argument inevitably happens in a church that treasures honesty and discernment, consensus is always possible in the light of our call to unity in Christ. When the call to purity is set against charity or humility, both Christian community and truth suffer. The tragic occasions of coercion in the church—both east and west—should caution us against taking too much pride in our interpretations of the gospel or our patterns of life. Theology is always provisional. In spite of the sharp rhetorical categories of orthodoxy and heresy, both negotiation and compromise were also part of historical catholicity in the early church.

All Christians belong to a community of faith that is continually challenged and chastened by the injustices of history. Following the path of self-offering initiated by Jesus guarantees conflict with society and within the church. Looking back at our history should encourage us that even the most painful crisis can be weathered and endured. The gospel is not easy, but it is ultimately secure in its freedom to follow a living God. In our corporate life, as in our individual journeys, we will at times become seekers whether we like it or not. Like the Christians who lived before us, we walk a pilgrim's path.

Endnotes

～ **Chapter One: Anglican Identity and Early Christian Traditions**

1. Irenaeus, *Against Heresies* 3.38.1, in *A New Eusebius*, ed. J. Stevenson and rev. W. H. C. Frend (Cambridge: Cambridge University Press, 1987), 113.

2. Quoted in Paul Avis, *Anglicanism and the Christian Church* (Minneapolis: Fortress Press, 1989), 42.

3. Ibid., 66.

4. Hymn 657 in *The Hymnal 1982*.

5. Quoted in *The Study of Anglicanism*, ed. Stephen Sykes and John Booty (Philadelphia: Fortress Press, 1988), 412.

～ **Chapter Two: The World of the Early Church**

1. Celsus, *On the True Doctrine* (altered), trans. R. J. Hoffman (New York: Oxford University Press, 1987), 74-75.

2. Origen, *Against Celsus* 8.72, trans. Henry Chadwick (Cambridge: Cambridge University Press, 1953), 507.

3. Tertullian, *Apology* 40.2, in *A New Eusebius*, 158.

4. Eusebius, *The Martyrs of Lyons and Vienne*, in *A New Eusebius*, 39-40.

5. *Epistle to Diognetus* (altered), in *A New Eusebius*, 55.

～ Chapter Three: Apostolic Christianity

1. Ignatius, *To the Smyrnaeans* 8, in *A New Eusebius*, 15.

2. *The Gospel of Truth*, in *The Nag Hammadi Library in English*, ed. J. Robinson, 3rd ed. (San Francisco: Harper & Row, 1988), 46.

3. *The Gospel of Truth*, 40-41.

4. Irenaeus, *Against Heresies* 3.19.6, in *A New Eusebius*, 119.

5. Ibid., 3.18.6, in *The Christological Controversy*, ed. and trans. R. A. Norris (Philadelphia: Fortress Press, 1980), 53.

6. Origen, *First Principles* 3.5.6, trans. G. W. Butterworth (Gloucester: Peter Smith, 1973), 242.

7. Irenaeus, *Against Heresies* 4.20.7 (altered), in vol. 1 of *The Ante-Nicene Fathers*, ed. A. Roberts and J. Donaldson (Grand Rapids: Eerdmans, 1981), 490.

8. Tertullian, *On the Soldier's Crown*, in *A New Eusebius*, 171-172.

9. Irenaeus, *Against Heresies* 4.33.8 (altered), in *The Ante-Nicene Fathers*, 1:508.

10. Tertullian, *On Purity* 21, in *Treatises on Penance*, trans. W. LeSaint, Ancient Christian Writers (Westminister: The Newman Press, 1959), 122.

11. *Fragments*, in *A New Eusebius*, 107.

12. Tertullian, *Prescription Against the Heretics* 7, in *A New Eusebius*, 167.

13. Irenaeus, *Against Heresies* 4.33.7 (altered), in *The Ante-Nicene Fathers*, 1:508.

～ **Chapter Four: Christianity and Social Crisis**

1. Cyprian, *On the Unity of the Catholic Church*, in *A New Eusebius*, 230.

2. Ignatius, *Letter to the Magnesians* 7, in *Early Christian Writings: The Apostolic Fathers*, trans. Maxwell Staniforth (Hammondsworth: Penguin Books, 1968/1987), 72.

3. *Didache* 9; also found in *The Hymnal 1982*, hymn 302.

4. Irenaeus, *Against Heresy*. 5.2.1-2 (altered), in *A New Eusebius*, 119.

5. Tertullian, *On the Soldiers' Crown*, in *A New Eusebius*, 171.

6. *Didache* 6 in *Early Christian Writings*, 193; *The Epistle to Barnabas* also has a contrast of the "Two Ways."

7. *Epistle to Diognetus* (altered), in *A New Eusebius*, 55-56. Part of this letter is also found in *The Hymnal 1982*, hymn 489.

8. Justin, *Apology* 1.16, in *A New Eusebius*, 59.

9. Galen, *Fragment*, in *A New Eusebius*, 137.

10. Tertullian, *To His Wife 4*, in *Treatises on Marriage and Remarriage*, tr. W. LeSaint (Westiminster: The Newman Press, 1956), 29.

11. Quoted by Augustine in *City of God*, trans. Henry Bettenson (New York: Penguin Books, 1972)19.23.

12. *The Martyrdom of Perpetua*, in *A Lost Tradition: Women Writers of the Early Church*, ed. Patricia Wilson-Kastner (Lanham, Md.: University Press of America, 1981), 22.

13. Eusebius, *The Ecclesiastical History*, trans. J. E. L. Oulton, Loeb Classical Library, 2 vol. (Cambridge: Harvard University Press, 1973) v. 2, 119

14. Cyprian, *Letter* 27.1 in *A New Eusebius*, 218.

15. Cyprian, *On the Unity of the Church*, in *A New Eusebius*, 229.

16. *Martyrdom of Perpetua* 13, in *A Lost Tradition*, 26.

～ Chapter Five: Imperial Christianity

1. *The Sayings of the Desert Fathers: The Alphabetical Collection* (altered), trans. Benedicta Ward (Kalamazoo: Cistercian Publications, 1975), 3.

2. From *The Sayings of the Desert Fathers*, in *Creeds, Councils, and Controversies*, ed. J. Stevenson and W. Frend (Cambridge: Cambridge University Press, 1989), 170.

3. Jerome, *Letter* 22, in *Creeds, Councils, and Controversies*, 167.

4. Ward, *Sayings of the Desert Fathers*, 157.

5. Ibid., 142.

6. Ibid., 193.

7. See Peter Brown, *The Cult of the Saints* (Chicago: University of Chicago Press, 1981).

8. This interpretation of Christian imperial art is the recent thesis of Thomas Mathews, *The Clash of Gods: A Reinterpretation of Early Christian Art* (Princeton: Princeton University Press, 1993).

9. See hymns 5, 14, 19, 21, 54, 55, and 233 in *The Hymnal 1982*.

10. John Chrysostom, *Baptismal Instructions*, trans. P. Harkins (Westminster: The Newman Press, 1963), 97.

11. Peter Brown, *Power and Persuasion: Towards a Christian Empire* (Madison: University of Wisconsin Press, 1992).

∾ **Chapter Six: Who is Jesus?**

1. Perpetua, *The Martyrdom of Perpetua* 4 and 12, in *A Lost Tradition: Women Writers of the Early Church*, ed. Patricia Wilson-Kastner (Lanham, Md.: University Press, 1981) 21,25.

2. Ignatius, *To the Romans* 7.2 (altered), in *The Ante-Nicene Fathers*, 1:76.

3. Felicitas, *The Martyrdom of Perpetua* 15, in *A Lost Tradition*, 27.

4. *Vision of Priscilla*, in *A New Eusebius*, 107.

5. Translation by R. G. Young in *Prayer from Alexander to Constantine*, ed. M. Kiley (London: Routledge, 1997), 317. See also *The Book of Common Prayer*, 118.

6. Quoted in Origen, *Against Celsus* 8.12, in *A New Eusebius*, 132.

7. Hippolytus, *Refutation*, in *A New Eusebius*, 148.

8. Hippolytus, *Against Noetus*, in *A New Eusebius*, 146.

9. Justin, *Apology* 2.13, in *A New Eusebius*, 62.

10. Tertullian, *Apology* 21, in *A New Eusebius*, 161.

11. Irenaeus, *Against Heresies* 3.2, in *The Christological Controversy*, 49.

12. Ibid., 5.1, in *The Christological Controversy*, 58.

13. Tertullian, *On the Flesh of Christ* 4.3, in *The Christological Controversy*, 68.

14. *Second Clement* 9.5, in *The Apostolic Fathers* v. 1, trans. K. Lake, Loeb Classical Library (Cambridge: Harvard University Press, 1975).

15. Athanasius, *Against the Arians* 3.33, in *The Christological Controversy*, 92.

ᴥ **Chapter Seven: Who is God?**

1. Gregory of Nyssa, *On the Son and Holy Spirit*, quoted in W. Frend, *The Rise of Christianity* (Philadelphia: Fortress Press, 1984), 636.

2. Athanasius, *Against the Arians* 1.21, in *The Trinitarian Controversy*, ed. W. Rusch (Philadelphia: Fortress Press, 1980), 85.

3. Ibid., 1.25, in *The Trinitarian Controversy*, 88.

4. Basil of Caesarea, *Letter* 159.2, in *Creeds, Councils, and Controversies* (Cambridge: Cambridge University Press: for SPCK, 1989), 83.

5. Gregory of Nyssa, *To Ablabius*, in *The Trinitarian Controversy*, 152.

6. Gregory of Nazianzus, *Letter* 101, in *Creeds, Councils, and Controversies*, 90.

ᴥ **Chapter Eight: The Church in Late Antiquity**

1. Robert Markus, *The End of Ancient Christianity* (Cambridge: Cambridge University Press, 1990).

2. Augustine, *Confessions of St. Augustine* 5.2, trans. R. Pine-Coffin (London: Penguin Books, 1961).

3. Augustine, *On the Trinity* 9.5, in *The Trinitarian Controversy*, 170.

Resources

∼ Church History

For Anglicanism and church history in general, see two volumes in this series: *The Anglican Vision* by James E. Griffiss and *Living with History* by Fredrica Harris Thompsett. Readable and readily available histories of early Christianity include *The Early Church* by Henry Chadwick (Harmondsworth: Penguin Books, 1967), *The Rise of Christianity* by W. H. C. Frend (Philadelphia: Fortress Press, 1984), and the two-volume *The Story of Christianity* by Justo L. González (San Francisco: Harper & Row, 1984). *The Oxford Illustrated History of Christianity* edited by J. McManners (Oxford: Oxford University Press, 1990) presents it all with wonderful illustrations.

To listen to the voices of the age itself, one can read many fine translations of ancient texts. *A New Eusebius* and *Creeds, Councils, and Controversies*, both edited by J. Stevenson and revised by W. H. C. Frend (Cambridge: Cambridge University Press for SPCK, 1966/1989) are collections of excerpts from the first to the sixth century; *Doctrine and Practice in the Early*

Church by Stuart Hall (Guildford: Biddles Ltd. for SPCK, 1991) is a companion history to be read with these volumes. *Sources of Early Christian Thought*, edited by William Rusch (Philadelphia: Fortress Press), are collections of texts on specific themes, such as Christology, Trinity, marriage, or the church. Several series provide extensive translations of individual authors: *Ancient Christian Writers, The Fathers of the Church*, and the reprint of the Victorian series, *The Ante-Nicene and Nicene Fathers*.

～ Romans, Jews, and Christians

This whole period may be best approached by reading Peter Brown's *The Rise of Western Christendom* (Oxford: Blackwell, 1996) or his *The World of Late Antiquity* (London: Thames and Hudson, 1971). Robin Lane Fox's massive *Pagans and Christians* (New York: Alfred A. Knopf, 1987) and Robert Wilken's *The Christians as the Romans Saw Them* (New Haven: Yale University Press, 1984) sympathetically present Roman religion. *Her Share of the Blessings* by Ross Shepard Kraemer (Oxford: Oxford University Press, 1992) discusses the role of women in all religions.

In *The Rise of Christianity* (Princeton: Princeton University Press, 1996), Rodney Stark offers a sociologist's view of the evidence and draws on recent work, including Wayne Meeks's *The First Urban Christians* (New Haven: Yale University Press, 1983). A fine dual history of Christians and Jews is *Christianity and Rabbinic Judaism*, edited by Hershel Shanks (London: SPCK, 1993). Novels that make the period come alive include *Julian* by Gore Vidal (New York: Random House/Vintage Books, 1962; 1967) and *The Beacon at*

Alexandria by Gillian Bradshaw (Boston: Houghton Mifflin company, 1986).

∼ Spirituality

Christian Spirituality, volume one, edited by Bernard McGinn (New York: Crossroad, 1987), offers articles on four centuries of spiritual practice and thought. Peter Brown's *Body and Society* (New York: Columbia University Press, 1988) is essential to understanding asceticism as a social and spiritual movement. Roberta Bondi's *To Love as God Loves* and *To Pray as God Prays* (Philadelphia: Fortress Press, 1987, 1991) are personal readings of the desert Christians. The series called Classics of Western Spirituality, published by Paulist Press, offer individual collections of the major authors, such as Gregory of Nyssa's *Life of Moses*, Augustine's *Confessions*, and Origen's *Commentary on the Song of Songs*.

A one-volume introduction to the history of liturgy is Herman Wegman's *Christian Worship in East and West* (Collegeville: The Liturgical Press, 1990). On transformations of art and architecture, see Thomas Mathew's *The Clash of Gods* (Princeton: Princeton University Press, 1993) and Richard Krautheimer's *Three Christian Capitals* (Berkely: University of Callifornia Press, 1983). On the cult of the martyrs see Peter Brown, *The Cult of the Saints* (Chicago: The University of Chicago Press, 1981) and Judith Perkins, *The Suffering Self* (London: Routledge, 1995).

∼ Theology

A general overview is provided by Frances Young in *The Making of the Creeds* (New York: Trinity

International Press, 1991) and a more detailed account in her *From Nicaea to Chalcedon* (Philadelphia: Fortress, 1983). To look in more detail upon the changing images of Christ, see Jaroslav Pelikan, *Jesus Through the Centuries* (New Haven: Yale University Press, 1985) and Glenn Chesnut, *Images of Christ* (Minneapolis: The Seabury Press, 1984).

Scholarship on Gnosticism is always changing: Kurt Rudolph's *Gnosis* (San Francisco: Harper & Row, 1983) is a good introduction, while Michael William's *Rethinking Gnosticism* (Princeton: Princeton University Press, 1996) is a major revision. An excellent introduction to western thought is *Augustine of Hippo* by Peter Brown (Berkely: University of California Press, 1967). For critical reflection on the development of doctrine, see *The Making of Christian Doctrine* by Maurice Wiles (Cambridge: University of Cambridge Press, 1967). Good introductory reading in ancient theologians includes Origen, *Contra Celsum* or Athanasius, *On the Incarnation*. The Library of Christian Classics includes volumes on *Alexandrian Christianity* and *Christology of the Later Fathers*.

Questions for Discussion

〜 Chapter One: Anglican Identity and
Christian Traditions

1. Everyone who studies history is attracted to some periods more than others. In your own view of the history of the church, are some periods more important than others? Which ones, and why?

2. This chapter talks about the appeal that the early church has traditionally held for Anglicans. Which traditions we have inherited from the early church are particularly important to you as an Anglican?

3. Much attention has been focused on diversity and inclusivity in the church today. Lyman notes that "the 'unity in multiplicity' of the ancient church offered an authoritative model" for Anglicanism at the time of the Reformation. In what ways do you think that is still true today?

～ Chapter Two: The World of the Early Church

1. This chapter describes how the Jesus movement arose out of a melting pot of religions—mystery religions, Judaism, Greek and Roman philosophy, Stoicism, and so on. What is your experience of relations between Christians and other religions?

2. In many parts of the world Christians are still persecuted. Have you ever experienced disapproval or even outright hostility because of your beliefs?

3. What parallels—social, political, economic—do you see between the world of the early church and the world today?

～ Chapter Three: Apostolic Christianity

1. Read through the Apostles' Creed (BCP 53/96), which is based on an early rule of faith. What does it say about God? Jesus? What does it *not* say? Why?

2. Over the years the church has debated again and again the question of orthodox belief versus heresy. How do you discern what is true in your faith? How does your own experience, your reading of scripture, or the tradition of the church fit into this process?

3. One of the ways the early church discerned orthodox beliefs was to ask whether a teacher was in line with the apostles. How do you decide which church leaders today are in agreement with "apostolic tradition"? Does it matter to you if they are?

⟶ **Chapter Four: Christianity and Social Crisis**
1. How do you think the history of the church would be different if the orders of ministry had remained more fluid and inclusive of women?

2. Fourth-century Christians worried over questions of moral purity and how closely ordinary people should be held to codes of conduct. Which do you think should matter most in the Christian life: purity or compassion? Why?

3. What role do you think spiritual gifts such as dreams or healing should play in modern faith?

⟶ **Chapter Five: Imperial Christianity**
1. Do you think Constantine's conversion and adoption of Christianity as the religion of the empire was good for the church, or not? Why?

2. Have you ever used spiritual disciplines to focus your life? What sorts of practices work best for you?

3. What qualities have you most admired in people of strong faith in your life? How would you recognize a holy person today?

⟶ **Chapter Six: Who is Jesus?**
1. Read the *Phos hilaron* from Evening Prayer (BCP 64/118). What does it tell us about who Jesus was to the early Christians?

2. Think about some striking images of Jesus you have seen in churches and museums, or heard in

scripture and the prayers of the church. Which have meant the most to you? Why?

3. What phrases or images would you use to describe the universal significance of Jesus in modern cultures?

～ Chapter Seven: Who is God?

1. Compare the Nicene Creed (BCP 358) to one of the eucharistic prayers (BCP 334-336/362-363). What similarities do you see? Differences? How does God act as Trinity in each of these texts?

2. When was the last time you disagreed with someone over theology? How did you come to a resolution?

3. This chapter describes the enormous investment that everyone from shopkeepers to bishops had in religious debate during the early centuries. Why do you think theology was such a passionate topic of discussion at all levels of Roman society? How do you think our understanding of salvation has changed over time?

～ Chapter Eight: The Church in Late Antiquity

1. If you were a Christian living in the fifth century, would you have agreed with the Donatists or with Augustine over the question of what to do with schismatics? Why?

2. Are all Christians called to be saints? What do you think it means to be a saint today?

3. What are some of the ways you think the church today has been shaped by the early church?

C owley Publications is a ministry of the Society of
St. John the Evangelist, a religious community
for men in the Episcopal Church. Emerging from the
Society's tradition of prayer, theological reflection,
and diversity of mission, the press is centered in the
rich heritage of the Anglican Communion.

Cowley Publications seeks to provide books, audio
cassettes, and other resources for the ongoing theological exploration and spiritual development of the
Episcopal Church and others in the body of Christ. To
this end, it is dedicated to developing a new generation
of theological writers, encouraging them to produce
timely, creative, and stimulating publications of excel-
lence, and making these publications available widely,
reaching both clergy and lay persons.